The Drug Enforcement Administration

KNOW YOUR GOVERNMENT

The Drug Enforcement Administration

Rebecca Stefoff

CHELSEA HOUSE PUBLISHERS

On the cover: A hidden camera captures the progression of a drug bust as it unfolds on the streets of New York.

Frontispiece: A suspected drug offender is led away by DEA agents in New York City.

Chelsea House Publishers
Editor-in-Chief: Nancy Toff
Executive Editor: Remmel T. Nunn
Managing Editor: Karyn Gullen Browne
Copy Chief: Juliann Barbato
Picture Editor: Adrian G. Allen
Art Director: Maria Epes
Manufacturing Manager: Gerald Levine

Know Your Government
Senior Editor: Kathy Kuhtz

Staff for THE DRUG ENFORCEMENT ADMINISTRATION
Assistant Editor: Karen Schimmel
Deputy Copy Chief: Nicole Bowen
Editorial Assistant: Elizabeth Nix
Picture Coordinator: Melanie Sanford
Picture Researcher: Dixon & Turner Research Associates, Inc.
Assistant Art Director: Loraine Machlin
Senior Designer: Noreen M. Lamb
Production Coordinator: Joseph Romano

Library of Congress Cataloging-in-Publication Data
Stefoff, Rebecca, 1951–
   The Drug Enforcement Administration / Rebecca Stefoff.
     p.   cm. — (Know your government)
   Bibliography: p.
   Includes index.
   Summary: Surveys the history, structure, and current functions of the Drug Enforcement Administration and describes its influence on modern society.
   ISBN 0-87754-849-8
   0-7910-0892-4 (pbk.)
   1. United States. Drug Enforcement Administration—Juvenile
literature. 2. Narcotics, Control of—United States—Juvenile literature. [1. United
States. Drug Enforcement Administration. 2. Narcotics, Control of.] I. Title.
II. Series: Know your government (New York, N.Y.)   89-9904
HV5825.S724   1989   CIP
353.0076′5—dc20   AC

CONTENTS

KNOW YOUR GOVERNMENT

The American Red Cross

The Bureau of Indian Affairs

The Central Intelligence Agency

The Commission on Civil Rights

The Department of Agriculture

The Department of the Air Force

The Department of the Army

The Department of Commerce

The Department of Defense

The Department of Education

The Department of Energy

The Department of Health and
Human Services

The Department of Housing and
Urban Development

The Department of the Interior

The Department of Justice

The Department of Labor

The Department of the Navy

The Department of State

The Department of Transportation

The Department of the Treasury

The Drug Enforcement Administration

The Environmental Protection Agency

The Equal Employment
Opportunities Commission

The Federal Aviation Administration

The Federal Bureau of Investigation

The Federal Communications Commission

The Federal Government: How it Works

The Federal Reserve System

The Federal Trade Commission

The Food and Drug Administration

The Forest Service

The House of Representatives

The Immigration and Naturalization Service

The Internal Revenue Service

The Library of Congress

The National Aeronautics and Space
Administration

The National Archives and Records
Administration

The National Foundation on the Arts
and the Humanities

The National Park Service

The National Science Foundation

The Nuclear Regulatory Commission

The Peace Corps

The Presidency

The Public Health Service

The Securities and Exchange Commission

The Senate

The Small Business Administration

The Smithsonian

The Supreme Court

The Tennessee Valley Authority

The U.S. Arms Control and
Disarmament Agency

The U.S. Coast Guard

The U.S. Constitution

The U.S. Fish and Wildlife Service

The U.S. Information Agency

The U.S. Marine Corps

The U.S. Mint

The U.S. Postal Service

The U.S. Secret Service

The Veterans Administration

CHELSEA HOUSE PUBLISHERS

INTRODUCTION

Government: Crises of Confidence

Arthur M. Schlesinger, jr.

From the start, Americans have regarded their government with a mixture of reliance and mistrust. The men who founded the republic did not doubt the indispensability of government. "If men were angels," observed the 51st Federalist Paper, "no government would be necessary." But men are not angels. Because human beings are subject to wicked as well as to noble impulses, government was deemed essential to assure freedom and order.

At the same time, the American revolutionaries knew that government could also become a source of injury and oppression. The men who gathered in Philadelphia in 1787 to write the Constitution therefore had two purposes in mind. They wanted to establish a strong central authority and to limit that central authority's capacity to abuse its power.

To prevent the abuse of power, the Founding Fathers wrote two basic principles into the new Constitution. The principle of federalism divided power between the state governments and the central authority. The principle of the separation of powers subdivided the central authority itself into three branches—the executive, the legislative, and the judiciary—so that "each may be a check on the other." The *Know Your Government* series focuses on the major executive departments and agencies in these branches of the federal government.

7

The Constitution did not plan the executive branch in any detail. After vesting the executive power in the president, it assumed the existence of "executive departments" without specifying what these departments should be. Congress began defining their functions in 1789 by creating the Departments of State, Treasury, and War. The secretaries in charge of these departments made up President Washington's first cabinet. Congress also provided for a legal officer, and President Washington soon invited the attorney general, as he was called, to attend cabinet meetings. As need required, Congress created more executive departments.

Setting up the cabinet was only the first step in organizing the American state. With almost no guidance from the Constitution, President Washington, seconded by Alexander Hamilton, his brilliant secretary of the treasury, equipped the infant republic with a working administrative structure. The Federalists believed in both executive energy and executive accountability and set high standards for public appointments. The Jeffersonian opposition had less faith in strong government and preferred local government to the central authority. But when Jefferson himself became president in 1801, although he set out to change the direction of policy, he found no reason to alter the framework the Federalists had erected.

By 1801 there were about 3,000 federal civilian employees in a nation of a little more than 5 million people. Growth in territory and population steadily enlarged national responsibilities. Thirty years later, when Jackson was president, there were more than 11,000 government workers in a nation of 13 million. The federal establishment was increasing at a faster rate than the population.

Jackson's presidency brought significant changes in the federal service. He believed that the executive branch contained too many officials who saw their jobs as "species of property" and as "a means of promoting individual interest." Against the idea of a permanent service based on life tenure, Jackson argued for the periodic redistribution of federal offices, contending that this was the democratic way and that official duties could be made "so plain and simple that men of intelligence may readily qualify themselves for their performance." He called this policy rotation-in-office. His opponents called it the spoils system.

In fact, partisan legend exaggerated the extent of Jackson's removals. More than 80 percent of federal officeholders retained their jobs. Jackson discharged no larger a proportion of government workers than Jefferson had done a generation earlier. But the rise in these years of mass political parties gave federal patronage new importance as a means of building the party and of rewarding activists. Jackson's successors were less restrained in the distribution of spoils. As the federal establishment grew—to nearly 40,000 by 1861—the politicization of the public service excited increasing concern.

After the Civil War the spoils system became a major political issue. High-minded men condemned it as the root of all political evil. The spoilsmen, said the British commentator James Bryce, "have distorted and depraved the mechanism of politics." Patronage, by giving jobs to unqualified, incompetent, and dishonest persons, lowered the standards of public service and nourished corrupt political machines. Office-seekers pursued presidents and cabinet secretaries without mercy. "Patronage," said Ulysses S. Grant after his presidency, "is the bane of the presidential office." "Every time I appoint someone to office," said another political leader, "I make a hundred enemies and one ingrate." George William Curtis, the president of the National Civil Service Reform League, summed up the indictment. He said,

> The theory which perverts public trusts into party spoils, making public
> employment dependent upon personal favor and not on proved merit,
> necessarily ruins the self-respect of public employees, destroys the
> function of party in a republic, prostitutes elections into a desperate
> strife for personal profit, and degrades the national character by lower-
> ing the moral tone and standard of the country.

The object of civil service reform was to promote efficiency and honesty in the public service and to bring about the ethical regeneration of public life. Over bitter opposition from politicians, the reformers in 1883 passed the Pendleton Act, establishing a bipartisan Civil Service Commission, competitive examinations, and appointment on merit. The Pendleton Act also gave the president authority to extend by executive order the number of "classified" jobs—that is, jobs subject to the merit system. The act applied initially only to about 14,000 of the more than 100,000 federal positions. But by the end of the 19th century 40 percent of federal jobs had moved into the classified category.

Civil service reform was in part a response to the growing complexity of American life. As society grew more organized and problems more technical, official duties were no longer so plain and simple that any person of intelligence could perform them. In public service, as in other areas, the all-round man was yielding ground to the expert, the amateur to the professional. The excesses of the spoils system thus provoked the counter-ideal of scientific public administration, separate from politics and, as far as possible, insulated against it.

The cult of the expert, however, had its own excesses. The idea that administration could be divorced from policy was an illusion. And in the realm of policy, the expert, however much segregated from partisan politics, can

9

never attain perfect objectivity. He remains the prisoner of his own set of values. It is these values rather than technical expertise that determine fundamental judgments of public policy. To turn over such judgments to experts, moreover, would be to abandon democracy itself; for in a democracy final decisions must be made by the people and their elected representatives. "The business of the expert," the British political scientist Harold Laski rightly said, "is to be on tap and not on top."

Politics, however, were deeply ingrained in American folkways. This meant intermittent tension between the presidential government, elected every four years by the people, and the permanent government, which saw presidents come and go while it went on forever. Sometimes the permanent government knew better than its political masters; sometimes it opposed or sabotaged valuable new initiatives. In the end a strong president with effective cabinet secretaries could make the permanent government responsive to presidential purpose, but it was often an exasperating struggle.

The struggle within the executive branch was less important, however, than the growing impatience with bureaucracy in society as a whole. The 20th century saw a considerable expansion of the federal establishment. The Great Depression and the New Deal led the national government to take on a variety of new responsibilities. The New Deal extended the federal regulatory apparatus. By 1940, in a nation of 130 million people, the number of federal workers for the first time passed the 1 million mark. The Second World War brought federal civilian employment to 3.8 million in 1945. With peace, the federal establishment declined to around 2 million by 1950. Then growth resumed, reaching 2.8 million by the 1980s.

The New Deal years saw rising criticism of "big government" and "bureaucracy." Businessmen resented federal regulation. Conservatives worried about the impact of paternalistic government on individual self-reliance, on community responsibility, and on economic and personal freedom. The nation in effect renewed the old debate between Hamilton and Jefferson in the early republic, although with an ironic exchange of positions. For the Hamiltonian constituency, the "rich and well-born," once the advocate of affirmative government, now condemned government intervention, while the Jeffersonian constituency, the plain people, once the advocate of a weak central government and of states' rights, now favored government intervention.

In the 1980s, with the presidency of Ronald Reagan, the debate has burst out with unusual intensity. According to conservatives, government intervention abridges liberty, stifles enterprise, and is inefficient, wasteful, and arbitrary. It disturbs the harmony of the self-adjusting market and creates worse troubles than it solves. Get government off our backs, according to the popular cliché, and our problems will solve themselves. When government is necessary, let it be at the local level, close to the people. Above all, stop the inexorable growth of the federal government.

In fact, for all the talk about the "swollen" and "bloated" bureaucracy, the federal establishment has not been growing as inexorably as many Americans seem to believe. In 1949, it consisted of 2.1 million people. Thirty years later, while the country had grown by 70 million, the federal force had grown only by 750,000. Federal workers were a smaller percentage of the population in 1985 than they were in 1955—or in 1940. The federal establishment, in short, has not kept pace with population growth. Moreover, national defense and the postal service account for 60 percent of federal employment.

Why then the widespread idea about the remorseless growth of government? It is partly because in the 1960s the national government assumed new and intrusive functions: affirmative action in civil rights, environmental protection, safety and health in the workplace, community organization, legal aid to the poor. Although this enlargement of the federal regulatory role was accompanied by marked growth in the size of government on all levels, the expansion has taken place primarily in state and local government. Whereas the federal force increased by only 27 percent in the 30 years after 1950, the state and local government force increased by an astonishing 212 percent.

Despite the statistics, the conviction flourishes in some minds that the national government is a steadily growing behemoth swallowing up the liberties of the people. The foes of Washington prefer local government, feeling it is closer to the people and therefore allegedly more responsive to popular needs. Obviously there is a great deal to be said for settling local questions locally. But local government is characteristically the government of the locally powerful. Historically, the way the locally powerless have won their human and constitutional rights has often been through appeal to the national government. The national government has vindicated racial justice against local bigotry, defended the Bill of Rights against local vigilantism, and protected natural resources against local greed. It has civilized industry and secured the rights of labor organizations. Had the states' rights creed prevailed, there would perhaps still be slavery in the United States.

The national authority, far from diminishing the individual, has given most Americans more personal dignity and liberty than ever before. The individual freedoms destroyed by the increase in national authority have been in the main the freedom to deny black Americans their rights as citizens; the freedom to put small children to work in mills and immigrants in sweatshops; the freedom to pay starvation wages, require barbarous working hours, and permit squalid working conditions; the freedom to deceive in the sale of goods and securities; the freedom to pollute the environment—all freedoms that, one supposes, a civilized nation can readily do without.

"Statements are made," said President John F. Kennedy in 1963, "labelling the Federal Government an outsider, an intruder, an adversary. . . . The United States Government is not a stranger or not an enemy. It is the people of fifty states joining in a national effort. . . . Only a great national effort by a great people working together can explore the mysteries of space, harvest the products at the bottom of the ocean, and mobilize the human, natural, and material resources of our lands."

So an old debate continues. However, Americans are of two minds. When pollsters ask large, spacious questions—Do you think government has become too involved in your lives? Do you think government should stop regulating business?—a sizable majority opposes big government. But when asked specific questions about the practical work of government—Do you favor social security? unemployment compensation? Medicare? health and safety standards in factories? environmental protection? government guarantee of jobs for everyone seeking employment? price and wage controls when inflation threatens?—a sizable majority approves of intervention.

In general, Americans do not want less government. What they want is more efficient government. They want government to do a better job. For a time in the 1970s, with Vietnam and Watergate, Americans lost confidence in the national government. In 1964, more than three-quarters of those polled had thought the national government could be trusted to do right most of the time. By 1980 only one-quarter was prepared to offer such trust. But by 1984 trust in the federal government to manage national affairs had climbed back to 45 percent.

Bureaucracy is a term of abuse. But it is impossible to run any large organization, whether public or private, without a bureaucracy's division of labor and hierarchy of authority. And we live in a world of large organizations. Without bureaucracy modern society would collapse. The problem is not to abolish bureaucracy, but to make it flexible, efficient, and capable of innovation.

Two hundred years after the drafting of the Constitution, Americans still regard government with a mixture of reliance and mistrust—a good combination. Mistrust is the best way to keep government reliable. Informed criticism

12

is the means of correcting governmental inefficiency, incompetence, and arbitrariness; that is, of best enabling government to play its essential role. For without government, we cannot attain the goals of the Founding Fathers. Without an understanding of government, we cannot have the informed criticism that makes government do the job right. It is the duty of every American citizen to know our government—which is what this series is all about.

Federal agents escort suspects apprehended in the Sicilian Connection raid to the federal courthouse in New York City. The March 1988 drug bust, one of the largest in U.S. history, climaxed a three-year joint investigation by the DEA, the FBI, and Italian law enforcement agencies.

ONE

The Drug War

The biggest drug bust in U.S. history took place early on the morning of March 31, 1988. On the 26th floor of New York City's Federal Building, supervisors of the Federal Bureau of Investigation (FBI) and the Drug Enforcement Administration (DEA) paced nervously in a dimly lit room that had been set up as a command center. Radios crackled and walls glowed with computer-controlled maps of the city streets.

As dawn approached, 260 FBI and DEA agents took up their positions and checked their weapons as they got ready to raid more than 40 homes and businesses in the New York area. In Boston, Washington, D.C., Charlotte, North Carolina, and Los Angeles, similar teams moved in on their targets. And across the Atlantic Ocean, law enforcement officials in Italy prepared to carry out raids precisely timed to coordinate with those planned for the United States. Their targets were secret criminal societies—called the N'Drangheta, the Cammora, and the Sicilian Mafia—that supply heroin, a powerful drug derived from the flower of the opium poppy, to criminal organizations in the United States.

At 4:10 A.M., the tension in the command center broke suddenly. "We got him," announced the leader of Arrest Team 24 over the two-way radio, reporting the first arrest of the night.

That was only the beginning. Within 25 minutes, the carefully prepared arrest teams had nabbed half of their targets. By 5:30 A.M., nearly all of the

15

suspects were in police custody. The grand total in the 2 countries was 200 arrests. No one was killed, but there were some difficult moments. One suspected drug dealer broke down in tears when an undercover agent who had pretended to be his friend pulled out a badge; another suspect's home was guarded by a fierce watchdog, but the suspect surrendered when the arresting agents threatened to shoot the dog. In Brooklyn, New York, a DEA agent had to run after a suspect's Lincoln for 300 yards; the suspect was not trying to escape—his chauffeur had panicked and had left the car in gear. The agent later compared the incident to the famous chase scene in the movie *The French Connection* but added that it was "much more realistic."

The investigation that climaxed that morning started in the fall of 1985, when 75 of the highest-ranking supervisors and agents in the FBI and the DEA met in Boston for a planning session. At that meeting, they decided to launch an all-out attack on the number one source of heroin in the United States: the Sicilian Mafia and its connections in U.S. criminal organizations. This so-called Sicilian Connection was believed to be smuggling at least $300 million worth of heroin—and perhaps even more—into the country each year.

The federal agents' goal was ambitious. They were not interested in arresting the street-corner drug addicts and the small-time drug dealers or even the more elusive middlemen who recruited couriers for international flights and set up drug buys over the phone. This time, they wanted to go to the top—to the highest levels in the network of heroin supply and distribution. To arrest these drug kingpins on charges that would hold up in court would require two extremely difficult and delicate strategies.

First, the FBI and DEA agents on the case would have to work closely with each other and with other narcotics investigation and law enforcement agencies, both in the United States and in Italy. State and local police would have to be in on the investigation, partly because their knowledge of local drug dealings might be a source of valuable clues and partly because they might inadvertently hamper the federal agents' progress if they were kept in the dark. Still more important, however, would be communication and cooperation with Italian law enforcement agencies. The Italians had given the FBI much of the information about the Sicilian Connection that was discussed during the Boston planning meeting, and the FBI would have to repay this courtesy by timing their own case to coincide with Italian investigations. If U.S. officials moved too slowly, for example, the Sicilian drug bosses might be warned in time to escape arrest. But if the agents moved too quickly, they might alarm the Sicilians into shutting down their operation temporarily to avoid arrest. Fortunately, law enforcement officials on both sides of the Atlantic realized that

16

An American delegation headed by Attorney General William French Smith meets with Italian government officials in January 1985 to discuss the connection between organized crime and international drug trafficking. That fall, high-ranking supervisors of the DEA and the FBI met in Boston to plan a daring undercover investigation of the Sicilian Mafia and its contacts in U.S. criminal organizations.

they could strike a harder blow against the heroin traffic if they pooled their resources and turned their two parallel investigations into a single international case.

The second important strategy in the attack on the Sicilian Connection would be undercover work. For the first time, the FBI and the DEA would try to place undercover agents wired with concealed microphones inside a major narcotics organization. Federal supervisors felt that undercover infiltration was the only way to obtain enough of the right kind of evidence against the Sicilians' American partners. But undercover work is the riskiest part of drug enforcement. And all undercover agents know the penalty for an infiltration attempt that goes wrong: Such failures can be fatal.

The investigation moved slowly at first. Throughout 1986, agents in offices around the country followed up hundreds of leads from informants and listened to thousands of hours of wiretapped phone conversations, trying to pin down the identities of the organization's major figures. Meanwhile, undercover

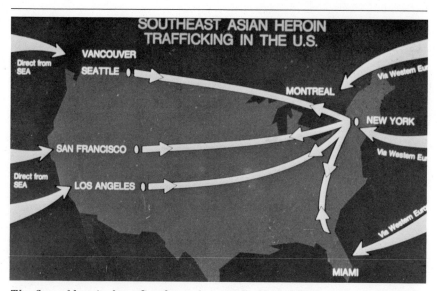

The flow of heroin from Southeast Asia to the United States takes numerous routes. Although heroin addiction in the United States has declined since its peak in the early 1970s, statistics show that its use is on the rise again.

agents played dangerous double games, posing as drug buyers, trying to work their way up the ladder from transactions with two-bit street dealers to direct contact with the big-time suppliers. In order to do so, they had to make big purchases to win the dealers' confidence and spark their greed. All in all, undercover agents working on the Sicilian Connection investigation made at least 15 heroin buys using government-supplied funds—sometimes as much as $200,000 per kilogram of heroin (1 kilogram is equal to 2.2046 pounds).

Finally, in early 1987, the investigators got their first big break. A routine comparison of field reports showed that a heroin dealer named Emanuele Adamita, who had escaped from prison in Italy and was being sought by the FBI in New York, had turned up in Florida, where he was trying to sell heroin to undercover DEA men. The FBI and the DEA began working closely together on the Adamita case, and before long their dealings with Adamita led them to the trail of a mysterious "guy in Brooklyn," as a very cautious supplier of heroin was called by the smaller drug peddlers. The agents suspected that this anonymous person was one of the major figures in the Sicilian Connection.

By July 1987, the narcotics agents had learned that the "guy in Brooklyn" appeared to be deeply involved in major heroin rings in North Carolina and in the New York City area. Then, by piecing together records of Adamita's

18

known contacts and those of some North Carolina and New York dealers, the federal law enforcement agents came up with a name: Alfredo "Tony" Spavento, a Brooklyn clothing dealer. Spavento was known to be involved in several criminal activities, but he was careful to avoid direct contact with drugs, and he did not like to do business with people he did not know well. Getting him to carry out a drug deal would not be easy.

An undercover FBI agent who had met Spavento went to work on him, pressuring the drug boss to sell him some heroin. On at least two occasions, heroin deals were set up but fell through at the last moment because Spavento became suspicious. On one occasion, instead of handing over the heroin, Spavento took the agent, who was wearing a concealed microphone, for an unexpected joyride to a spot 80 miles out of New York City. FBI backup men followed a few miles behind, listening to their radios, afraid of hearing the agent say the code word that meant Spavento was going to kill him. But Spavento brought the undercover agent back unharmed. A few weeks later, Spavento introduced the agent to 2 men who sold him a kilogram of heroin for $195,000. The FBI and the DEA now had the evidence they needed to arrest Spavento and his henchmen.

They were unable to move right away, however, because the investigation had taken some new and shocking twists. Agents discovered that Spavento and Adamita, among others in the United States, were working with their Italian partners to open up a whole new branch of the drug trade. The drug cocaine, which is produced from the leaves of the coca plant, is plentiful in the United States but comparatively scarce in Europe, where it sells for even higher prices than in America. The Sicilian Connection wanted to set up a two-way flow in which the Italians would supply heroin to the United States in return for cocaine, which would then be marketed in Europe. In a telephone conversation tapped by federal law enforcement officials, one of Spavento's partners talked about opening Italy to large-scale cocaine dealing. "If we could do that," he said enthusiastically, "we could make money by the shovelful. By the *shovelful!*"

This plan horrified the Italian drug enforcement authorities, who asked the FBI and the DEA for help. In order to find out more about the plan, Spavento's undercover contact offered to make cocaine available. Prospects for the arrangement looked so promising that Spavento took the agent to Rome to discuss the venture with his partners. Nothing of the plan materialized, but the agent was able to confirm the suspicions of the Italian authorities about the identities of some of the Roman members of the Sicilian Connection. As a result, the Italians began infiltrating Italy's criminal organizations with their own undercover drug agents.

Finally, in March 1988, both the American and the Italian investigations had progressed far enough. The time had arrived to call in the undercover agents, arrest the suspects, and begin the long process of prosecution. It will no doubt be years before the hundreds of cases that began that March day have made their way through the plea bargainings, hearings, trials, and appeals that lie ahead. (In a plea bargain, the defendant in a lawsuit agrees to plead guilty to lesser charges to avoid being tried for more serious crimes.) Agents who spent months undercover in the field will spend more months in courtrooms,

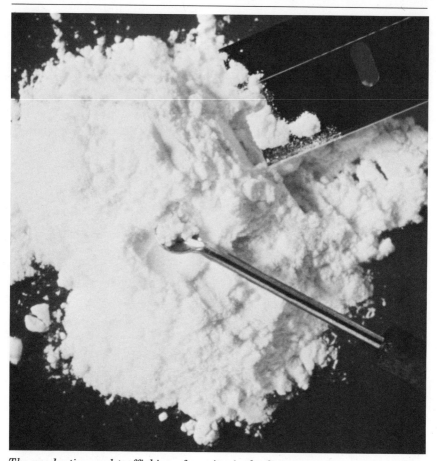

The production and trafficking of cocaine is the fastest-growing segment of the illegal drug trade. This powerful narcotic is derived from the leaves of the Erythroxylon coca *shrub, which is native to the Andes mountain region of South America.*

testifying before attorneys, judges, and juries, trying to put the drug bosses behind bars. And new investigations are already under way. The drug agents who broke up the Sicilian Connection know that the flow of heroin into the United States continues. At best, the biggest drug bust in history did no more than slow the heroin traffic for a while. As long as drug dealers can dream of making money by the shovelful, plenty of dealers will be waiting to take the place of each one who is stopped.

A Business and a Battlefield

The illegal drug trade is big business in the United States and around the world. No one is sure exactly how big a business it is because drug traffickers do not pay taxes on their trade or keep public records. Governments, law enforcement agencies, and groups such as the United Nations' World Health Organization (WHO), which advises and trains people in health administration and coordinates projects to combat widespread disease, try to estimate the volume of illegal drugs produced, the number of users, and the dollar value of the drug traffic. Their results vary widely, however, especially on the international level. Yet most sources agree on these basic facts:

- The amount of illegal drug material produced each year is increasing, as is the number of users.

- Some of the world's poorest nations obtain a substantial part of their earnings in foreign currencies through the drug trade. This is true of cocaine in parts of Latin America, of opium in parts of Southeast Asia and west Asia, and of cannabis (the marijuana plant) in parts of south and west Asia. Enforcement of antidrug laws is difficult in countries where drug crops may bring in much of the farmers' basic income.

- Cocaine production and trafficking is the fastest-growing segment of the illegal drug trade. In 1987, an estimated 400,000 acres were devoted to illegal cultivation of the coca plant, the source of cocaine. This figure has been increasing by about 10 percent each year.

- Estimates of international cocaine production vary widely, ranging from 200 tons to as much as 800 tons in 1987, but the DEA can confirm about 400 tons of cocaine produced in 1987. More than half of this amount was consumed in the United States, much of it in the form of crack, a less expensive but powerfully addictive cocaine preparation. About 1,600 Americans died as a result of cocaine use in 1987. That same year, the number of people admitted

Turkish women sow the seeds of opium poppies, the source of the narcotics opium, morphine, and heroin. Drug crops generate important revenues in some developing countries, where they frequently provide a major portion of the farmers' basic income.

to U.S. hospital emergency rooms for conditions connected with cocaine increased by 86 percent.

- The production and consumption of opium products such as heroin is increasing. The production and consumption of cannabis products such as marijuana and hashish has remained fairly steady since the mid-1970s. The illegal use of hallucinogens (synthetic or naturally occurring drugs that cause hallucinations, or illusions of seeing something that does not exist), amphetamines (drugs that act as stimulants on the central nervous system), barbiturates (drugs such as sleeping pills that are derived from barbituric acid and that have a tranquilizing or calming effect on the body), and other drugs that the government has placed under federal control has also remained steady since the mid-1970s.

- The United States has about 1.2 million drug addicts and about 23 million people who use drugs on a casual, or "recreational," basis. At least 1 in every 10 newborn babies in the United States has been exposed to illegal drugs through its mother.

- American users spend more on illegal drugs each year than the country's top-earning corporation earns during the same period. Between 1981 and 1988, the federal and state governments spent $21 billion of taxpayers' money on drug law enforcement and prevention programs.

- Drug abuse is directly related to crimes, including at least 25 percent of all murders, 40 to 50 percent of all robberies and burglaries, and more than 30 percent of all criminal offenses in the United States. A hard-core heroin or crack addict commits an average of 200 property crimes each year.

To those who deal in illegal drugs, the drug trade is a business. To the top drug bosses, it is a far-flung and hugely profitable international enterprise. To the corner crack dealer or the teenager peddling pills at school, it is a job that often pays for the dealer's own drug habit. But society at large views the drug trade in other ways.

Every president since Richard M. Nixon has called for action against the individual, social, and economic destruction that has accompanied the increase in drug use. In the 1970s, it became common for drug use to be called a "plague" or a "disease," a reflection of society's recognition of drug addiction as a medical disorder rather than a criminal activity. But in the 1980s, under the influence of President Ronald Reagan, the U.S. government exchanged medical images for military ones to describe the drug problem. Drugs are no longer viewed as an infection in the body of society: They are an enemy. And American antidrug activities are now referred to as the "war on drugs."

The Drug Enforcement Administration

The federal government's frontline soldiers in the war on drugs are the 5,050 employees of the DEA. The DEA, which is part of the Department of Justice, is the leading federal agency for drug law enforcement. Its principal responsi-

A heroin addict convicted for burglary does time in a New York jail. Drug abuse is directly related to crime, including at least 40 to 50 percent of all robberies and burglaries.

Attorney General Richard Thornburgh (left) discusses the details of a multinational drug enforcement operation as DEA assistant administrator Tom Kelly looks on. Effective action in the "war on drugs" often involves cooperation by police at the local, national, and international levels.

bility is to fight the war on drugs at the highest possible level by identifying and bringing to justice the major drug offenders who are involved in drug trafficking across state lines or between nations.

The DEA is also responsible for overseeing the legal drug, or pharmaceutical, industry in the United States, for managing a national narcotics information system, and for representing the United States in cooperative drug enforcement programs with the United Nations and foreign countries.

Effective attack or defense in the war on drugs usually requires a combination of weapons. Even the DEA rarely acts alone. Instead, most of its cases are interagency activities such as the one involving the Sicilian Connection, in which it teamed up with the FBI. Since 1982, in fact, the director of the FBI has supervised the activities of the DEA, so the two agencies usually work together on drug cases. The DEA also works closely with the U.S. Customs Service; the U.S. Coast Guard; the Bureau of Alcohol, Tobacco and Firearms;

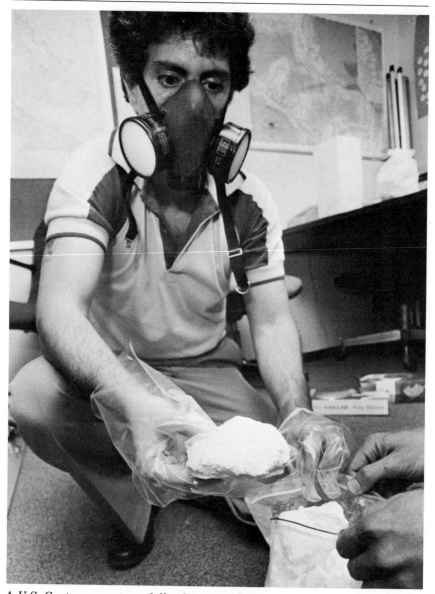

A U.S. Customs agent carefully places a small amount of confiscated cocaine in sealed bags to be used as evidence and as lab samples. Most of the DEA's investigations are interagency activities that bring together such organizations as the FBI, the U.S. Customs Service, and the Food and Drug Administration.

the Food and Drug Administration (FDA); state and local police forces across the country; drug law enforcement officials and police in other nations; and the International Criminal Police Organization (Interpol), a multinational organization that coordinates the exchange of information between the criminal investigation departments of its member nations.

Federal drug laws—and the need for someone to enforce them—appeared only in the 20th century. The DEA is young, as federal agencies go, having been formed only in 1973. Although the history of drug enforcement before that date is not lengthy, it reflects dramatic changes both in patterns of drug use and in society's views about drugs.

A fragment from an Assyrian frieze depicts a man holding a poppy plant. Many ancient cultures cultivated the opium poppy, the sap of which was highly prized for its painkilling and mind-altering properties.

TWO

Early
Enforcement Efforts

Drug use has long been a part of human life. Nearly all cultures have made and consumed some form of alcoholic drink, and tea and coffee, which contain the stimulant caffeine, have been staple beverages in large areas of the world for centuries. But among the substances that figure in today's war on drugs, the first to be widely used was probably the narcotic opium, which is made from the sap of a flower called the opium poppy.

Opium was known to the ancient Near Eastern civilizations of Mesopotamia and Egypt. The cultivation and use of the opium poppy had spread to Greece by the 9th century B.C. In the *Iliad*, an epic poem about the Trojan War believed to have been written in the 8th century B.C., the poet Homer mentions a drink that contained a drug. Scholars believe that this drink was probably a form of *soma* (an opium-based beverage that sometimes also contained alcohol), which was known to many Asian cultures.

Opium cultivation and use also spread eastward from the Mediterranean region into the lands that are now Iran, Afghanistan, Pakistan, and India. Knowledge of opium reached China in about the 7th century A.D., and in the following centuries the production and use of opium became entrenched in Southeast Asia, especially in the region that is now Burma, Laos, and Thailand. Opium cultivation reached Japan in the 15th century.

29

For hundreds of years Indians living in the Andes mountains of Peru, Bolivia, and Ecuador have grown and harvested coca. Although these Indians traditionally chew coca leaves to dull the discomforts of hunger, cold, and fatigue, the booming cocaine trade has transformed the plant into an important cash crop.

Almost equally ancient and widespread is the use of marijuana and hashish, intoxicating drugs made from the *Cannabis sativa* plant, which is a form of hemp. The plant grows in many parts of the world, and the drugs it yields have been used for centuries by some members of European, North African, and Asian cultures.

The world's third major drug-producing plant, a shrub called *Erythroxylon coca*, is the source of the stimulant and painkiller cocaine. Coca has been used as a drug in parts of western South America since at least 1500 B.C. Peruvian, Bolivian, and Ecuadoran Indians who live at high altitudes in the Andes mountains have traditionally chewed coca leaves as a stimulant to dull the discomforts of cold, hunger, thirst, and fatigue. To the north, some Native American cultures in Central and North America have used hallucinogenic drugs from plants, such as the fruit of the peyote cactus, in religious ceremonies.

Traditional, widespread drug use, however, occurred almost exclusively in Asia, Africa, and South America. A combination of climate and history made drug use almost unknown in Western Europe and the United States. In the 17th, 18th, and 19th centuries, Western nations seeking to expand their

British naval forces attack Chinese ships during the First Opium War in 1841. Despite Chinese efforts to prevent British merchants from expanding their opium trade into China, the British were eventually victorious, and opium flooded the Far East.

31

empires and their trade markets encountered the drug customs of other cultures. For the most part, Americans and Europeans considered drugs to be a legitimate object of commerce, like any other commodity, and they exploited the Asian opium trade, some reaping huge profits. They thought that the use of drugs was simply the result of moral weaknesses or cultural flaws in what they believed were the "backward" peoples of the world. Few, if any, Western opium merchants or their contemporaries imagined drug abuse as a growing social evil that could attack a whole nation.

The Chinese knew better. Fearful of the damaging effects of widespread opium addiction on society, the Chinese government outlawed the drug in 1729. From 1833 on, treaties between China and the United States barred U.S. citizens from taking part in the drug trade in the Far East. But the British were eager to expand their lucrative trade in Indian opium into China. Great Britain attacked China and, after the Opium Wars of 1839–42 and 1856–58, crushed the Chinese resistance. Opium flooded the Far East. By that time, however, the heyday of the legal drug trade was almost at an end, and the Western world was on the verge of a new view of drugs.

A Growing Threat

Just a few years after the British fought to expand the opium trade into China, people in Europe and the United States were beginning to develop drug habits of their own.

Opium had become readily available in the Western world in the form of pills or laudanum, a mixture of alcohol and opium. It appeared in many medicines and health drinks, including many children's medicines. In the early 1800s, scientists discovered how to chemically produce morphine, a strong sedative and anesthetic, from opium. Doctors prescribed this new drug for everything from cancer to colds, and the abundance of narcotics soon generated a wave of new problems. (Technically, narcotics are habit-forming drugs that produce unconsciousness or sleep or reduce pain. In law enforcement, however, the term is generally used to refer to opium- or coca-based drugs, even though the latter are often more stimulating than relaxing in their effect.) Thousands of people in all walks of life suffered from what was called the "opium sickness"— dependency on or addiction to opium. And doctors discovered to their dismay that the morphine they had been prescribing so freely was powerfully addictive. In the 1890s, German, British, and American scientists discovered

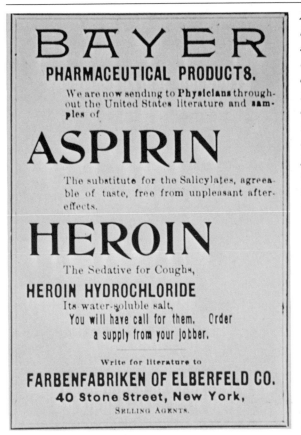

An advertisement for heroin-laced cough syrup manufactured by the Bayer Pharmaceutical firm. In the 1800s and early 1900s opium, morphine, and heroin were hailed as cures for everything from cancer to colds and were frequently added to a variety of commercial medicines and health drinks.

how to make heroin from morphine. Ironically, doctors hailed heroin as a nonaddictive substitute for morphine.

Although opium and the chemicals made from it were the leading drugs at the turn of the century, cocaine—first manufactured from coca leaves by German scientists in 1862—had also appeared in the United States and Europe. In the 1880s, U.S. doctors tried to use cocaine as a cure for opium addiction and alcoholism. Like opium, it was added to a number of nonprescription medicines and beverages—including, until about 1903, the soft drink Coca-Cola. Cocaine also became popular in Europe, where Sigmund Freud, the founder of psychoanalysis, recommended it as a cure for morphine addiction. Sherlock Holmes, the popular fictional detective created by British physician and novelist Sir Arthur Conan Doyle, is depicted in a book published in 1888 as injecting himself with cocaine. This novel, *The Sign of Four*, gave cocaine a touch of literary style—although Holmes's sidekick and medical adviser, Dr. Watson, strenuously urged the detective to give up the habit. "Count the cost!" Watson says to Holmes in the opening pages."Your brain may, as you say, be roused and excited, but it is a pathological and morbid process which involves increased tissue change and may at least leave a permanent weakness. And you know what a black reaction comes upon you. Surely the game is hardly worth the candle."

Watson was fictional, but real people also spoke up against cocaine. Claims that it could cure opium, alcohol, and morphine addiction were soon disproved,

In 1909, President Theodore Roosevelt (center) arranged for the leaders of the foremost drug-producing and drug-consuming nations to meet in Shanghai, China, to discuss the problem of the burgeoning narcotics business. Three years later world leaders met again at The Hague in the Netherlands, where they drafted an international drug agreement known as the Hague Opium Convention to control the production and distribution of narcotics.

and victims of a new addiction appeared. In 1887, a *Washington Post* article carried the headline "The Cocaine Habit," the forerunner of hundreds of headlines that would appear in the nation's newspapers and magazines a century later.

By the early 1900s, the medical profession and the general public had become alarmed by the hazards of narcotics addiction. During the first years of the 20th century, a number of states passed laws that required stricter controls on medical prescriptions for narcotics.

President Theodore Roosevelt, one of the first U.S. leaders to take action against drugs, believed that international measures were needed to control the flow of narcotics. Coca, which had been transplanted from South America to a few locations in Indonesia, and opium, which had been transplanted to Mexico, were not cultivated in the United States. Yet the country was becoming one of the world's major consumers of narcotics.

Roosevelt wanted the nations that produced narcotics and those that were threatened by narcotics consumption to work together to police the drug trade. In 1909, he arranged a meeting in Shanghai, China, at which representatives of 13 nations, including some—but not all—of the narcotics producers, discussed the problem. Three years later, at a second meeting known as the Hague Opium Convention because it was held at The Hague, in the Netherlands, the participating nations signed an international agreement to try to restrict the distribution of narcotics.

The Hague Convention called on its members to limit their production of opium and coca products to medical uses and to control the import and export of raw opium and coca leaves. It was the first of dozens of international agreements, treaties, and programs aimed at controlling the production and distribution of narcotics and other drugs—efforts that have not succeeded in stamping out or even curbing the traffic in illegal drugs. Many experts claim, however, that a true long-term victory in the war on drugs will require global drug policy and enforcement. In the meantime, the United States has been fighting its own battle against drugs, both at its borders and within them, ever since the Hague Opium Convention.

U.S. Drug Law and Enforcement

The first federal drug law in the United States was the Harrison Narcotics Act of 1914. In form, the act was little more than a tax measure: It charged a federal tax of one cent per ounce on imported opium and coca products and required everyone who shipped, handled, sold, or prescribed these products to register with the government and to keep records of their transactions. From the outset the act was interpreted quite strictly. No one outside the medical profession could obtain a registration to deal in narcotics, and doctors could be arrested if they prescribed drugs for addicts, rather than as part of other medical treatment.

Once the law was passed, it had to be enforced. Because the Harrison Act was primarily a tax act, the Internal Revenue Service (IRS), part of the Treasury Department, assumed the job of enforcing the law. In 1915, 162 agents and collectors in the Miscellaneous Division of the IRS were assigned responsibility for "restricting the sale of opium," as their official orders read under the Harrison Act. This was the first federal drug enforcement attempt, and those 162 tax officers were the direct ancestors of today's DEA.

In 1919, the Treasury Department estimated that there were 1 million narcotics addicts in the United States. The Harrison Act made it difficult or impossible for them to obtain drugs from their doctors. Although the government operated narcotics clinics in some communities from 1918 to 1923, providing minimum supplies of drugs to addicts in an effort to detoxify them (or at least to allow them to satisfy their dependency without criminal activity), an increasing number of users and addicts turned to new sources: drug smugglers and peddlers. The connection between drugs and crime grew stronger. The agents who were assigned to drug enforcement under the Harrison Act reported that the trade in smuggled narcotics was bigger than anyone had suspected and was growing fast. But as Treasury officials tried to attack the problem, they were hit with new problems caused by Prohibition.

In 1919, the states ratified the Eighteenth Amendment to the Constitution, sometimes called the Prohibition amendment, which banned the manufacture, transport, and sale of alcoholic beverages in the United States. That same year Congress passed the National Prohibition Enforcement Act, also known as the Volstead Act (after Andrew J. Volstead, the Minnesota congressman who wrote the legislation), which outlawed beverages containing more than one-half of one percent alcohol and charged the Treasury Department with the responsibility for arresting those who violated the new liquor laws.

Enforcing Prohibition was a massive task, doomed to failure. It fell to the IRS, which immediately formed a Prohibition Unit. The drug enforcement agents from the Miscellaneous Division were assigned to the Prohibition Unit, which, with only 1,550 agents, was drastically understaffed. Nevertheless, the unit struggled to carry on a twofold attack on liquor smugglers, who were called bootleggers, and drug smugglers. Often the two were the same, as

Rumrunners intercepted by U.S. Treasury agents walk down a New York City dock in 1931. Enforcing Prohibition was a nearly impossible task that fell to the Internal Revenue Service and, later, to the Bureau of Prohibition.

An illicit opium den in New York City's Chinatown in 1925. In 1919, when the states ratified the Eighteenth Amendment to the Constitution, prohibiting the manufacture and sale of alcoholic beverages, many Americans took to buying liquor—and drugs—from bootleggers and drug smugglers associated with the world of organized crime.

many of the sea captains who turned their boats to the task of shipping illegal whiskey and rum to the United States later branched out into cocaine, morphine, and heroin smuggling. These small-time bootleggers and smugglers were soon driven out of business or were dominated by criminal organizations, such as those operated by Al Capone in Chicago and by Dutch Schultz and Legs Diamond in New York City.

Drug abuse increased during Prohibition, partly because the enormously widespread practice of buying bootleg liquor introduced thousands of people in all social classes to underground or criminal transactions and made it easier for them to experiment with drugs. Cocaine, in particular, gained greatly in popularity, but heroin, morphine, and marijuana use also increased. Cocaine use was associated with the new movie industry in California and with wealthy socialites and nightclubs. Marijuana use was sometimes linked to black urban centers, such as Harlem and New Orleans, and, later, to jazz musicians.

In 1927, the Treasury Department created the Bureau of Prohibition, separate from the IRS. The bureau was responsible for alcohol and drug law enforcement. In the tradition of interagency cooperation that is continued by the DEA today, agents of the bureau worked with state and local police to control illegal smuggling and dealing.

The Treasury Department took another step in drug enforcement just three years later, when it created a separate agency for narcotics control. Called the Bureau of Narcotics, this new agency concentrated on the drug trade. In 1933, Prohibition was repealed by the Twenty-first Amendment to the Constitution, but the Bureau of Narcotics was given greater power and responsibility by several new federal drug laws. The Marijuana Tax Act of 1937 placed marijuana and hashish in the category of illegal, federally controlled drugs. The Boggs Act of 1951 and the Narcotic Control Act of 1956 created harsher penalties for convicted drug users, including mandatory prison sentences. Under this act, dealers who were convicted of selling heroin to people under the age of 21 could face the death penalty.

By the mid-1960s, these enforcement measures had produced some results. The number of narcotics addicts in the country had decreased to about 600,000, and 15 percent of all prisoners in federal prisons were jailed on drug charges. But the drug enforcement system was severely strained in the late 1960s, when huge numbers of baby boomers (people born in the late 1940s and early 1950s) began experimenting with drugs. Marijuana use skyrocketed, and new drugs of abuse, including the hallucinogens lysergic acid diethylamide (LSD) and mescaline, as well as new types of amphetamines and barbiturates, entered the scene. Some of these, such as LSD, were completely illegal, manufactured in secret chemical laboratories. Others, such as some of the amphetamines and barbiturates, were legally produced drugs that were diverted from medical use through theft or fraud.

The federal government responded to the increasing drug traffic by combining the Bureau of Narcotics with the Food and Drug Administration's

John E. Ingersoll (left), director of the Bureau of Narcotics and Dangerous Drugs (BNDD), and BNDD regional director Daniel P. Casey exhibit a stash of heroin that was seized in a May 1972 raid in New York City. Although only 3 of the plastic packages shown contained heroin—the rest were filled with quinine and milk sugar—264 pounds of the drug were confiscated in a simultaneous raid in Belgium.

Bureau of Drug Abuse Control to form a new agency, the Bureau of Narcotics and Dangerous Drugs (BNDD). The agency's name showed that it had broadened its target beyond the traditional opium and coca narcotics. And it was no longer an offshoot of the Treasury Department. It was placed within the Justice Department, which is entirely devoted to arresting and prosecuting violators of federal laws, so that its activities could be directed by the U.S. attorney general. With the establishment of the BNDD, the drug war was about to enter a new phase.

Robert Stutman (left), director of the DEA's New York division, Andrew Maloney (center), U.S. Attorney, and Benjamin Ward (right), police commissioner of New York City, stand behind nearly $20 million and several sawed-off shotguns captured in a 1989 drug raid. Eleven suspects thought to be connected with a Colombian drug cartel were also apprehended in the January 5 raid, which was one of the largest cash hauls in the history of the war on drugs.

THREE

New Defenses

The next big step in America's antidrug battle came in 1970, when Congress passed the most recent of the major U.S. drug laws, the Comprehensive Drug Abuse Prevention and Control Act. Usually called the Controlled Substances Act, this legislation is still the basis of the federal war on drugs. The law enforcement aspects of this war are carried out under two sections of the act that are known as Title II and Title III. (Title I is a statement of the principle behind the Controlled Substances Act: The United States will regulate the traffic of drugs that it considers dangerous by means of a "closed distribution system," or in other words, by monitoring the manufacture, import, export, and distribution of all dangerous drugs and their raw materials.)

The act divides drugs into five categories, or schedules. Each drug is assigned to one of these schedules based on the answers to three questions: How dangerous is the drug? How great is its potential for abuse? And does it have any legitimate medical value?

A drug's dangerousness can involve several factors. One is the likelihood that its use will lead to death or injury. Another is the degree to which it causes addiction or psychological dependence, which is known as habituation.

The drug's abuse potential has to do with how plentiful it is, how easily it may be obtained, and how popular it is or may become. Pure opium, for example, is highly dangerous because it is so addictive. But its abuse potential is lower than that of cocaine or heroin because it is extremely rare in the United States. This is because producers of opium find it more profitable to process the crop into heroin rather than to sell it in its natural form. On the other hand, some very common drugs, such as aspirin, have a low abuse potential because they do not produce intoxicating or stimulating effects.

The third consideration in assigning drugs to the five schedules is their medical value. Dangerous drugs that have high potential for abuse but that offer some benefits in properly supervised medical treatment are listed in a schedule different from those that have no accepted medical value.

The most dangerous drugs—those with no accepted medical use in the United States and with a very high potential for abuse—are contained in Schedule I and include heroin, LSD, marijuana, peyote, mescaline, psilocybin, and methaqualone.

Dried marijuana leaves, marijuana cigarettes, and paraphernalia used for smoking marijuana. Marijuana has been used to treat people suffering from cancer and the eye disease glaucoma; however, its medical value is still being investigated, and it remains a Schedule I drug.

Undercover DEA agent Michael Levine (left) negotiates a 100-kilogram co-caine deal with Colombian drug traffickers in 1982. Colombia is the leading producer of cocaine, a Schedule II drug that, though it possesses some medi-cal value, is at the top of the DEA's list of illicitly sold narcotics.

Schedule II, like Schedule I, contains drugs that have a high potential for abuse and that can cause severe physical or psychological dependence: cocaine, opium, morphine, codeine, phencyclidine, methadone, methamphetamine, and others. These drugs may have medical uses under close supervision. Schedule I and II drugs are considered to cause the most serious health and criminal problems.

Schedule III contains substances that have a lesser potential for abuse than those in Schedules I and II, including some compounds with small amounts of narcotics. Paregoric, a liquid medicine that relieves diarrhea and intestinal pain and that contains some opium, is in Schedule III. Drugs in this schedule are available by prescription only.

Schedule IV contains drugs that have a lesser potential for abuse than those of Schedule III. This schedule includes the barbiturates, or sleeping pills, and diazepam, the tranquilizer that is marketed under the brand name Valium. Schedule IV drugs are available by prescription only.

Schedule V contains substances that have a lesser potential for abuse than those of Schedule IV. Medicines with minute amounts of opium or codeine are found in this schedule. Such preparations are generally prescribed to control coughing or diarrhea. Some Schedule V drugs may be purchased without a prescription.

More than 20,000 drugs or compounds are covered by the Controlled Substances Act. New drugs can be added, and drugs can be moved from one schedule to another if medical research supports the change. For example, amphetamines, which were found to be more addictive than originally thought, were moved from Schedule III to Schedule II in 1975. The painkiller propoxyphene hydrochloride, marketed under the brand name Darvon, was added to Schedule IV of the list of controlled substances in 1977. Since 1971, the DEA, working with the Food and Drug Administration and the National Institute on Drug Abuse, has labeled 28 drugs as controlled substances, moved 9 drugs to different schedules, and decontrolled 5 drugs, among them some forms of the pain reliever ibuprofen, which is found in such over-the-counter drugs as Advil and Nuprin and was deemed to be nonaddictive and nontoxic in small doses in 1984.

Each schedule carries its own set of federal penalties for illegal trafficking. A first offense involving a Schedule V drug, for example, carries a maximum 1-year prison sentence and a $10,000 fine. For a Schedule I or II drug, the penalties are more severe: 20 years in prison and a $250,000 fine for 5 grams or more of LSD or 1 kilogram or more of cocaine—for the first offense. Second

A DEA agent escorts 1 of 22 airline employees suspected of helping smuggle millions of dollars in cocaine through Miami International Airport in 1986. Under the Controlled Substances Act the maximum penalty for a first offense for cocaine trafficking is 20 years in prison and a $250,000 fine.

offenses can bring jail sentences of 40 years for a Schedule I drug or 6 years for a Schedule IV drug.

Schedules II through V also have individual sets of federal regulations that govern the manufacture, distribution, and storage of the listed drugs. (Schedule I drugs may not be prescribed for any reason.) For example, Schedule II drugs may be prescribed but may not be refilled; a second dispensation can be obtained only if a physician writes another prescription for the drug. Schedule III and IV drugs may be prescribed with up to five refills, and some Schedule V drugs may be purchased without a prescription. All in all, the Controlled Substances Act guides the government's entire strategy against the illegal use of drugs, from research to investigation to arrest to sentencing.

Only moments after President Richard M. Nixon signed the Comprehensive Drug Abuse Prevention and Control Act on October 27, 1970, he turned the law over to Attorney General John Mitchell (right), who, as head of the Justice Department, directed the federal drug-law enforcement effort. The act, which is generally referred to as the Controlled Substances Act, sets guidelines for the distribution of more than 20,000 drugs and establishes penalties for persons convicted of illegal trafficking.

Focus on Enforcement

The passage of the Controlled Substances Act highlighted that the drug problem had become a major political issue. It stimulated a boom in the creation of new drug-related agencies, committees, and organizations. The agents of the Bureau of Narcotics and Dangerous Drugs continued to serve as federal police, but other groups also became involved in stemming the drug trade. Three of the most important of these groups were formed in 1972: the Office of National Narcotics Intelligence, the Office of Drug Abuse Law Enforcement—both part of the Justice Department—and the Narcotics Advance Research Management Team of the executive branch of the government.

All of these groups collected data on drug use, researched drug abuse prevention methods and treatment programs, and carried out law enforcement measures—or at least made lengthy studies of enforcement measures and recommendations for improving them. The U.S. Customs Service, which is part of the Treasury Department, also had a special Drug Investigations Unit to deal with drug smuggling, and the FBI was increasingly involved with drug enforcement as the links between organized crime and the drug trade were revealed.

It quickly became apparent that the proliferation of drug-related agencies had led to an administrative mess. Time and effort were being wasted as researchers or investigators in two or more agencies duplicated each others' efforts, often unknowingly. Likewise, uncertainty and disagreements among the various groups as to who was in charge of what caused confusion and frustration. The federal antidrug effort was lively but fragmented. In 1973, President Richard M. Nixon approved a plan to reorganize and streamline this effort for greater efficiency.

The Drug Enforcement Administration was created in July 1973 under Presidential Reorganization Plan Number 2. The agency combined the responsibilities and staffs of five earlier agencies: the Bureau of Narcotics and Dangerous Drugs, the U.S. Customs Service Drug Investigations Unit, the Office of National Narcotics Intelligence, the Office of Drug Abuse Law Enforcement, and the Narcotics Advance Research Management Team. Like the majority of the agencies it replaced, the DEA was part of the Justice Department. The head of the DEA, whose title was administrator, reported to the U.S. attorney general, the head of the Justice Department. Through the attorney general, the DEA was charged with leading the attack on illegal trafficking both within the United States and abroad.

A U.S. Customs inspector surveys packages of hashish that were smuggled into the country inside the panels of a foreign-made van. Because narcotics are often secretly conveyed into the United States via manufactured goods and smugglers posing as ordinary travelers, the U.S. Customs Service maintains a special Drug Investigations Unit to try to stop the international drug flow.

Since its establishment in 1973, the DEA has undergone only one significant organizational change. On January 21, 1982, Attorney General William French Smith gave the FBI shared authority and responsibility with the DEA over drug offenses. Since then, the administrator of the DEA has reported to the director of the FBI, who in turn reports to the attorney general.

(continued on page 54)

In January 1982, Attorney General William French Smith announced that the DEA and the FBI would share authority and responsibility concerning drug offenses. Since then, the administrator of the DEA has reported to the director of the FBI, who in turn reports to the attorney general.

The Kings of Coke

Cocaine is the country's number one drug enemy, according to the DEA. In their attempts to make a dent in the flow of coke into the United States, DEA agents track pushers to their sources, and then track those sources to *their* sources. Over the course of hundreds of investigations, the DEA has put together a picture of how the multibillion-dollar international coke trade works.

Most of the illicit coca is grown in Bolivia and Peru—experts estimate that at least half of the world's coca comes from a single valley, the Huallaga, in Peru. But the leaves end up in Colombia, which dominates cocaine production and smuggling. The Colombian drug bosses are organized into rings, or "families," that are called cartels, each with its own network of chemists, accountants, gunmen, and other personnel.

Once a shipment of cocaine is ready for sale, the cartel's transportation crews take charge. These crews smuggle the cargo into the United States by land, sea, or air. They change routes, carriers, and methods of concealment frequently in order to slip past the U.S. Customs Service. Then, once a drug cargo has made it past customs—and most of them do—it is turned over to an off-load crew. The off-loaders are responsible for getting the cocaine from the point of entry into the hands of the next link in the chain, the brokers. The off-loaders, who are used to divert suspicion from the transportation crews, work for either the cartels or the brokers.

Brokers are individuals, nearly always operating within a criminal organization, who arrange for the sale and distribution of the cocaine to wholesale dealers throughout the country. The wholesalers then sell the cocaine, either to small-time, independent retail dealers or directly to users.

At each step of the process, the coke is cut—that is, diluted with other substances to increase its total volume and value. In late 1988, a kilogram of coca cost $500 in Peru; another $4,000 worth of chemicals and labor was needed to turn it into cocaine. That kilogram of cocaine could be sold to a U.S. wholesaler for $10,000 to $25,000; a European

Colombian drug kingpin Pablo Escobar Gaviria, photographed shortly before he went into hiding in 1984.

wholesaler would pay as much as $45,000. But when sold on the retail level, the kilogram would earn 10 times its wholesale price—or more.

The cartels generally take their profits from the wholesalers. The drug money is turned over to collectors known as bagmen. Then it is returned to the cartels, most often as direct cash deliveries, or through complicated systems of deposit and transfer in foreign banks. Sometimes the drug dollars are laundered by being passed through banks or through businesses owned by the cartels. Certain pizzerias or video-rental stores, for example, may report high annual earnings even though few pizzas or videotapes left the premises—the dollars came from drug sales.

The two largest cocaine cartels in Colombia are centered in the cities of Medellín and Cali. People refer to the cartel leaders, such as Pablo Escobar Gaviria of Medellín, as *magicos*, meaning "magicians." These men are indeed powerful. Bad things happen to anyone who interferes with them: The Medellín and Cali cartels together are believed to have been involved in the assassinations of a Colombian attorney general, at least 30 judges, and hundreds of law enforcement officials. The United States has repeatedly asked Colombia to extradite Pablo Escobar—that is, to send him to the United States to face criminal charges. So far, the Colombian government has refused.

One *narco-traficante*, as the coke kings are called in Colombia, was not

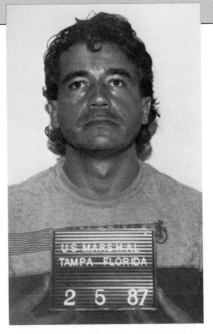

Carlos Lehder Rivas, a former cocaine king who is serving life plus 135 years in an Illinois federal prison.

so lucky. He is Carlos Lehder Rivas, a native of Colombia who moved to New York City as a teenager and took up drug smuggling, with connections to the Medellín cartel. Lehder was a showy, violent man who boasted that drugs would destroy America. "Cocaine is the Third World's atomic bomb," he said in 1985. He is thought to have smuggled 3.3 tons of cocaine into the United States between 1978 and 1980 and to have earned $250 million to $300 million doing it. Most of the money has vanished into the shadowy underground world of the drug trade, but Lehder's whereabouts are known. Arrested by the DEA and extradited from Colombia in 1987, he is serving life plus 135 years at a maximum security federal prison in Marion, Illinois.

(continued from page 50)

The principal reason for this change was to avoid duplication of effort and to make the most efficient use of agents and information. The FBI has always been in charge of investigations that involve organized crime associations or syndicates, and the Justice Department decided to concentrate its efforts on large-scale organized drug traffickers. In placing all federal drug enforcement activity under the overall supervision of the FBI director, Smith hoped for three results: that the FBI would benefit from the DEA's skills and experience when dealing with criminal cases involving drugs; that the DEA would benefit from the FBI's skills and experience when dealing with drug cases involving criminal organizations; and that the two agencies would accomplish more if they cooperated and did not get in each other's way.

These results have been achieved, but not without some costs. Organizations, like individuals, do not enjoy being demoted, and that was how many DEA people viewed the change in organization. It was difficult for DEA employees, both in administrative offices and in field investigations, to start taking orders from the FBI, especially because the two agencies have sometimes been involved in rivalries or disputes over authority. In addition, drug agents—particularly those who work undercover—have a reputation for independence. Some members of both the FBI and the DEA have resented sharing "their" cases. But the benefits of unified administration of the antidrug war far outweigh these issues, and, over time, the two agencies have worked together with increasing smoothness, as the Sicilian Connection case demonstrated.

Targeting the Enemy

The drug trade is so enormous, the abusers so numerous, and the problem so pervasive that the authorities have admitted that it will probably be impossible to end illegal drug trafficking completely. The DEA knows that it cannot police the world with only 2,800 agents. Therefore, its goal is to use these agents where they can do the most good: to reach the highest sources of supply and to seize the largest possible amounts of the most dangerous illicit drugs before they reach the market.

To do this, the DEA examines all of the information available about each drug violator it is investigating. It then uses a system called the Geographic Drug Enforcement Program (G-DEP) to classify each violator according to the type and amount of the drug involved, the area affected by the criminal operation, and the violator's position in the criminal organization. The most important

DEA special agents hone their skills at a firing range. The more than 5,000 employees of the DEA are the frontline soldiers in the nation's war on drugs.

offenders are placed in Class I, the lowest-level offenders in Class IV. For example, someone who peddles marijuana cigarettes around a neighborhood would belong to Class IV, but someone who directs the smuggling of pounds of cocaine through an international airport would belong to Class I.

This does not mean that drug enforcement officials condone local or small-time drug dealing. Indeed, they would like to arrest the neighborhood pot peddler *and* the international coke smuggler. But because the enforcement and justice systems do not have enough resources for both, drug officials must give priority to the most serious violators. The G-DEP system allows the DEA to take aim at the biggest targets.

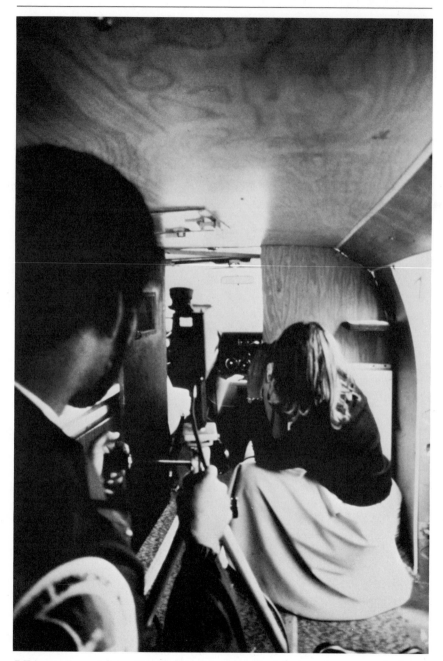

DEA agents watch an illegal drug buy from the interior of an unmarked van.

FOUR

Inside the DEA

In broad terms, the DEA's mission is to attack the illicit drug trade. The DEA breaks down that overall mission into the following five general areas of activity:

- Investigating major violators at the interstate and international levels, including arresting the violators and supporting their prosecution with testimony.
- Enforcing federal laws that govern the legal manufacture, distribution, and sale of controlled substances.
- Managing a national intelligence and information system for use in drug enforcement.
- Working with other federal law enforcement authorities, state and local authorities, drug enforcement counterparts in foreign nations, and international organizations such as Interpol and the U.N. Commission on Narcotics, which coordinates information about drugs and sponsors antidrug training programs.
- Maintaining training and research programs to support drug enforcement.

These activities are carried out by a total staff of 5,050 people. Slightly more than half of these DEA employees—2,800 of them—are special agents, the investigators responsible for most of the field work, including undercover operations and raids. Of the rest, some 1,200 are clerks or technicians in fields such as computer operations or communications; 550 are lawyers, administrative officers, or other professional specialists, including the 150 chemists who analyze evidence in the DEA's laboratories; 300 are diversion investigators, who focus on cases that involve the diversion of legally manufactured medical drugs for illegal sale or abuse; and 200 are intelligence specialists, who sift the thousands of scraps of information that find their way into the DEA's computers and files, looking for the patterns and connections that can predict trends or break cases.

The DEA tries to spread its forces as widely as it can. The agency's headquarters and the office of the administrator are located in Washington,

Chemists at a DEA laboratory analyze confiscated drugs. Approximately 150 scientists carry out important behind-the-scenes research at the DEA's 7 forensic science laboratories, where they examine fingerprints, test drugs, develop photographs, and perform other technical work.

DEA and U.S. Customs agents inspect a shipment of cocaine seized in Miami, Florida, in 1982. The DEA's Miami office, one of 19 division offices nationwide, is also one of the busiest.

D.C. Domestic field offices are located around the country. They are of three types: division offices, district offices, and resident offices.

The DEA has partitioned the nation into 19 divisions, which are the agency's principal administrative units. Each division has a central office that reports to the DEA's national headquarters. These division offices are located in Atlanta, Boston, Chicago, Dallas, Denver, Detroit, Houston, Los Angeles, Miami, Newark (New Jersey), New Orleans, New York, Philadelphia, Phoenix, San Diego, San Francisco, Seattle, St. Louis, and Washington, D.C. Alaska is included in the Seattle division, Hawaii and Guam in the Los Angeles division, and Puerto Rico and the Virgin Islands in the Miami division. The Miami division also includes three Caribbean offices that are considered domestic even though they are located on foreign soil: Kingston, Jamaica; Nassau, the Bahama Islands; and Santo Domingo, Dominican Republic.

The 19 divisions are subdivided into smaller administrative territories, which are covered by a nationwide total of 5 district offices and 96 resident offices. (The district offices are somewhat larger than the resident offices, which may consist of just two or three people.) Each district or resident office reports to the nearest division office.

The DEA's attempts at eliminating the illegal drug trade span the globe as well as the country. Under various international treaties and agreements, it maintains offices in 62 cities in 42 foreign countries. Some countries, such as Egypt and Japan, have only one DEA post. But countries in which drugs are grown or processed in large volume usually have more than one post. Colombia and Pakistan each have four offices; Thailand has three; Bolivia, Ecuador, and France each have two; and Mexico, which has been producing increasing amounts of heroin from homegrown opium poppies, has six.

Because successful investigations and prosecutions often depend on quick and accurate analysis of the drugs that are bought or seized by DEA and FBI agents, the DEA operates seven forensic science laboratories around the country. Working in these labs, the agency's forensic scientists—chemists and other people whose work is guided by legal or police needs—analyze drugs, examine fingerprints, and develop photographs. In addition, it is becoming increasingly common for the forensic chemists to accompany field teams of special and undercover agents on raids. The chemists are specially trained to dismantle criminal laboratories safely and to carry out meticulous vacuum sweeps of cars, rooms, and clothing to detect the tiniest traces of drugs.

The seven regional forensic laboratories are located in New York, Washington, D.C., Miami, Chicago, Dallas, San Francisco, and San Diego. They provide forensic science help not just to the DEA and the FBI but also to state and local authorities. An eighth DEA lab is located in McLean, Virginia. It is called the Special Testing and Research Laboratory, and it provides forensic services to the DEA's foreign offices and to the international organizations and foreign governments with which the DEA cooperates on investigations. This lab also backs up the regional labs when they encounter work overloads or tricky analyses.

A highly specialized type of drug analysis is performed at McLean. It is called drug ballistics because it is similar to the science of ballistics, which in law enforcement refers to the study of the firing, flight, and identification of bullets. Drug ballistics is the science of using microscopically precise measurements and chemical analyses of powders or pills to identify their source. A drug ballistics expert can tell whether two amphetamine tablets confiscated on

A small amount of cocaine is carefully examined at the Special Testing and Research Laboratory in McLean, Virginia, where a type of drug analysis known as drug ballistics is performed. This highly specialized science involves the use of microscopically precise measurements and chemical analyses of powders or pills to identify a substance's source.

opposite sides of the country were stolen from the same pharmaceutical corporation or whether two vials of cocaine seized on opposite sides of the world were manufactured in the same secret lab deep within the Colombian jungle. Such information helps the DEA trace the flow of drugs and connect the dealers to their contacts in the cartels and crime syndicates.

DEA Departments

Between the administrator at the head of the organization and the special agents in the field, the DEA's administrative organization consists of a number of specialized departments, which are called offices. Each has responsibility for some part of the agency's overall mission.

A Bolivian official talks to a gathering of coca growers about the legal and illegal aspects of coca production. Among antidrug efforts sponsored by the Bolivian and U.S. governments are those aimed at convincing farmers to grow other, legal crops.

The Office of Chief Counsel is the DEA's legal staff. Members of this office advise federal, state, and local prosecutors on the handling of drug cases and also represent the DEA and its agents if civil lawsuits are filed against them or if they are charged with crimes. The Office of Congressional and Public Affairs handles communication with the nation's lawmakers and the public. The Board of Professional Conduct sets standards for the behavior of agents and other employees and investigates any accusations of misbehavior by DEA personnel. These departments are not large. They are located in Washington, D.C., and report directly to the administrator.

Most of the agency's employees around the world belong to three much larger organizational groups called divisions: the Planning and Inspection Division, the Operational Support Division, and the Operations Division. Each of these divisions contains several specialized offices or other subdivisions and each is headed by an assistant administrator, who reports to the administrator of the DEA.

The Planning and Inspection Division is responsible for long-term planning of the DEA's programs and activities, for setting goals, and for reviewing and evaluating the agency's performance. It includes the Office of Professional Responsibility, which monitors the agency for any sign of illegal or questionable behavior. This office is something like an internal police unit that enforces the rules set by the Board of Professional Conduct.

The Operational Support Division is responsible for personnel matters, accounting, and purchasing supplies and equipment. It is the clerical and administrative backbone of day-to-day operations. This division includes the Office of Science and Technology, which runs the regional forensic laboratories and the Special Testing and Research Laboratory.

The Operations Division contains the real meat and potatoes of investigation and enforcement. Operations runs all of the domestic and foreign field offices, and all special agents and other field operatives belong to this division. The Operations Division includes the Office of International Programs. Among other activities, this office works with government and law enforcement authorities in foreign drug-producing countries to promote two antidrug programs. One is crop eradication, the destruction of coca, opium, or marijuana plants by chemical spraying or fire. The other is crop substitution, which encourages or pays farmers to grow other, legal crops. Two highly specialized units, the Office of Intelligence and the Office of Diversion Control, are part of the Operations Division as well.

Office of Intelligence

In the world of law enforcement, the term *intelligence* has the same meaning that it has in espionage. It refers to the gathering of information, sometimes by secret or devious means, to use against an enemy. The DEA's Office of Intelligence gathers information from a myriad of sources: reports from field agents; published statistics from around the world; communications from foreign drug enforcement officials; and reports from state and local police, the FBI, the U.S. Central Intelligence Agency (CIA), the Food and Drug Administration (FDA), the U.S. Customs Service, and the National Institute on Drug Abuse (NIDA). (NIDA, which is one of the National Institutes of Health, conducts and supports research on the physical, mental, and social effects of drug addiction and abuse and assists other federal agencies, state and local organizations, hospitals, and volunteer groups in planning, creating, and maintaining drug abuse programs.)

This information is recorded, sifted, collated, and studied by intelligence specialists, who use the material in two broad ways. One is to guide and support current investigations and programs. For example, one team of specialists monitors the Asian heroin trade and keeps a list called "The Top Ten Asian Heroin Violators," which is updated regularly and tells the field agents where to concentrate their efforts. The G-DEP program of violator

A DEA employee (second from right) inspects the facilities of a corporate drug-processing plant to ensure that the security system is adequate to prevent the illegal diversion of drugs produced by the company. Diversion, or theft of legally manufactured drugs, can occur at any point in the distribution process, from the first shipment of raw materials to a pharmaceutical plant to the dispensing of prescription medicines by a pharmacist.

classification is carried out by such teams of specialists. The other use of intelligence is in long-range forecasting and planning. For example, forthcoming opium and coca harvests are estimated, based on information such as weather reports and infrared satellite photographs of the fields. The DEA shares intelligence of this sort with other law enforcement agencies, both in the United States and abroad.

Office of Diversion Control

Under the Controlled Substances Act, the DEA's mission is not only to keep illicit drugs from entering the country but also to prevent drugs that are legally manufactured for medical use from being diverted for illegal use. The enforcement of this directive requires the Office of Diversion Control to obtain annual registrations from the more than 750,000 doctors, pharmacists, and hospital workers who handle or prescribe drugs in the United States. The office collects several million dollars in annual registration fees from these sources. The Office of Diversion Control also investigates and monitors drug manufacturers and wholesale drug distribution companies to make sure that they have adequate security systems and that their operations are crime free. In addition, it investigates cases of diversion—that is, cases in which drugs are obtained for illegal use by fraud or theft. Diversion can occur at any point, from the first shipment of raw materials to a pharmaceutical plant to the dispensing of prescription medicines by a corner pharmacist. As in all of its investigation and enforcement efforts, the DEA concentrates on large-scale diversions, trying to operate as close to the illicit drug source as possible. It also guides state and local law enforcement authorities in procedures for diversion control at the smaller, local level.

Office of Training

The Office of Training, a separate department within the DEA, designs and administers a variety of training programs to meet the needs of anyone, from a new agent to a foreign official. Until the late 1980s, most of the DEA's training took place at the Federal Law Enforcement Training Center (FLETC) in Glynco, Georgia. After 1987, however, DEA training was gradually consolidated with FBI training, which is carried out at the large federal training

(continued on page 68)

A Life Undercover

Drug agents and other law enforcement officers agree that one part of their job is more dangerous, more difficult, and more demanding than any other: undercover work. An undercover agent works his or her way into a drug ring or distribution network by pretending to be a dealer or buyer of illegal drugs. Once on the inside, the agent is in a position to report on the identities and activities of the people he or she encounters in the drug business. But he or she is also in a position of deadly danger if any criminal associates find out who the agent really is. The biggest breakthroughs in antidrug investigations come from undercover work. So do most deaths of agents on the job.

Undercover work is a fine art. The undercover agent cannot *act* the part of a dealer or buyer—he or she must *live* it, for the agent is essentially a spy in an enemy camp. An agent's clothing, language, and behavior must reassure the always-suspicious dealers that he or she is one of them. Many federal drug agents today receive training in undercover techniques—training that may save their life—from a man named Michael Levine, perhaps the most successful undercover agent the war on drugs has known. His story is told in a biography called *Undercover: The Secret Lives of a Federal Agent*, by Donald Goddard, published in 1988 by Times Books.

Levine grew up in the Bronx, New York, where he learned to mingle easily with local black and Hispanic street gangs. Tough and streetwise, he was often embroiled in fistfights—usually defending his younger brother, David. Once out of school, Levine joined the air force. Later, married and out of the ser-

Michael Levine (left), the master of undercover disguise.

vice, he served as an investigator in the Treasury Department, the Bureau of Alcohol, Tobacco and Firearms, and the U.S. Customs Service. During these years, he perfected an undercover technique, drawing on his ability to imitate accents and on his familiarity with the streets. He usually worked with an informer (that is, someone inside a criminal gang who gives evidence to the police or to federal agents either for money or to avoid prosecution), and he often ran six or seven cases at once, sometimes using several different identities.

Levine's 23-year undercover career set new standards for this kind of work. In 1970, he infiltrated a group of motorcycle gangs in New York State, lived with them for 3 months, and finally captured 4,000 sticks of dynamite that the bikers were planning to sell to terrorists in New York City. In 1971, he worked on an international case that made undercover history: He became the first agent to bring down the courier (in New York City), the traffickers (in Florida), *and* the heroin source (in Bangkok, Thailand) in a single case. A year later, he arrested Claude Pastou, a smuggler of heroin and cocaine, known as the French Connection. Levine brought his skills to the DEA when it was formed in 1973. A routine case against a pill dealer 2 years later led Levine's undercover character to 26 other arrests and scores of other offenders. The case remains the biggest undercover operation in the history of the DEA in terms of the

In 1970, Levine posed as a motorcycle gang member and confiscated explosives destined for terrorists.

number of cases and offenders brought in by a single contact.

Over the years, Levine has posed as a priest, a Mafia soldier, a Puerto Rican gang member, a Colombian drug dealer, and many other characters. He has brought more than 3,000 criminals to trial—more than any other drug agent. But he has also suffered the unavoidable personal stress of the undercover life: loneliness, frustration, fear for his life and that of his family, and the deterioration of his marriage because of his prolonged absences and 24-hour responsibilities. The relentless force that drives his personal war on drugs, however, is a powerful one. His younger brother, David, whom Levine had protected on the streets of their childhood, became a heroin addict and finally killed himself, saying, "I can't stand the drugs any longer." Michael Levine cannot stand them either.

DEA agents receive instruction in the martial arts as part of their basic training. Since 1987, the DEA and the FBI have carried out joint training at the federal training center at Quantico, Virginia.

(continued from page 65)

center in Quantico, Virginia. The facilities at Quantico include classrooms, weapons ranges, gymnasiums, and a detailed replica of an illicit drug lab so that agents can learn how to identify such labs and handle the chemicals and equipment they contain.

DEA special agents, diversion control investigators, intelligence specialists, and other employees receive both basic and advanced training, including occasional refresher courses to introduce seasoned agents to new equipment and methods. But the DEA also provides training for FBI agents who will be working in drug enforcement. In return, the FBI trains DEA agents in the special techniques of investigating organized crime. One of the DEA's most active programs involves training selected state and local police in drug enforcement techniques. Some of these individuals attend courses at Quantico, but each division has one or more agents assigned to teach classes and seminars within the division. The DEA provides some form of special training to an average of 6,400 federal, state, and local officials each year.

Another important aspect of training is international. An average of 1,000 foreign law enforcement officers from many countries receive DEA training each year. Some of these officers attend courses at Quantico; the DEA has agents who can teach in a variety of foreign languages. In addition, the DEA has three traveling teams that are available to give specialized, on-the-spot drug enforcement training in any part of the world. These mobile teams are sponsored by the State Department. They are designed to help give field agents in other nations the skills and the motivation to join the DEA in its attack on the global drug trade.

The Making of a Drug Agent

Many of the DEA's special agents—and a number of its other employees as well—have transferred to the DEA from other federal agencies, such as the FBI or the Bureau of Alcohol, Tobacco and Firearms. But the DEA also fills agent positions from the general public. Many candidates who apply for such positions come from law enforcement, military, or legal backgrounds.

Candidates must be between the ages of 21 and 35, pass physical and eye examinations, and have a valid driver's license. They also must possess certain qualifications of experience and/or education: three years of general working experience; or two years of specialized legal, military, police administration, or law enforcement experience; or a bachelor's degree from an accredited college or university; or certification as a public accountant. Candidates with greater qualifications—either three years of general experience and two years of specialized experience or a master's degree in a specialized field such as law enforcement or police administration—may be considered for positions at a higher grade, or salary, level.

A candidate who possesses acceptable qualifications and meets the physical and age requirements faces two further tests. One is an interview with a panel of DEA officials, to which the candidate must travel at his or her own expense. The interview is designed to test some of the candidate's personal qualities, such as reaction to stress and ability to communicate. The final test is an intensive background investigation of the candidate. Investigators may question friends, employers, or others about the candidate's personality and way of life. They check military, school, and police records. A candidate who is found to have a criminal record—even for minor offenses, such as driving violations— may be disqualified. Any form of drug abuse, no matter how long ago it occurred, results in automatic disqualification. But a candidate who passes muster may be selected to become a special agent.

Only a few of the candidates who apply for the position of special agent will get to wear the DEA badge. The requirements for acceptance are stiff, and anyone with a history of drug use—no matter how minor—is automatically disqualified.

All new special agents start their DEA careers with basic training, an intensive 15-week course at Quantico. Classes usually have about 40 members. Men and women receive identical training, including hand-to-hand combat and the use of handguns, rifles, shotguns, machine guns, and tear gas.

The course covers a multitude of topics: the Controlled Substances Act; drug chemistry and the effects of drugs; legal guidelines for search and seizure and the arrest and prosecution of suspects; interrogation techniques (how to get information from a suspect, either alone or with a partner); preparation of case reports; intelligence gathering and analysis; surveillance techniques (how to follow a suspect as well as how to avoid being followed); how to find and use informants within the criminal world; how to investigate wide-ranging and complex conspiracies; and undercover work (how to use a disguise, set up a false identity, and infiltrate a drug ring).

Trainees must complete this course successfully in order to remain in the DEA. Those who do are assigned to their first posts. DEA agents must be willing to accept any assignment, anywhere in the world, at any time. Most agents will return to Quantico or other federal training facilities from time to time for special or advanced training in foreign languages, diversion control, intelligence, forensic chemistry, or the DEA's newest advanced course: financial investigation techniques used to track drug fortunes through the labyrinth of secret bank accounts, cash laundering, foreign investments, and computerized money manipulation.

The life of a DEA agent is not easy or glamorous, and often it is outright dangerous. Yet for the men and women who make up the DEA's cadre of special agents, the perils of the job are overruled by the ardent desire to stamp out the illicit drug trade.

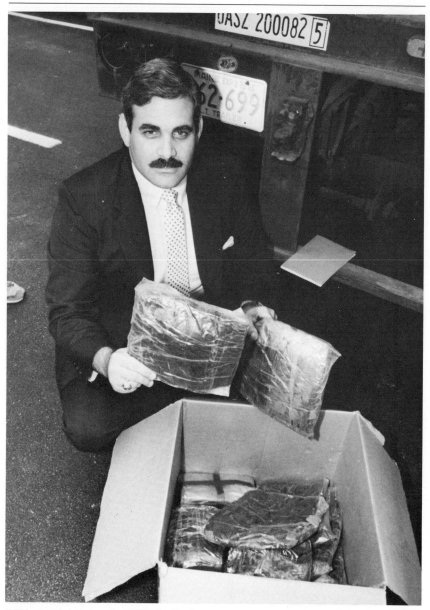

DEA special agent Jack Hook displays part of a 2,500-pound shipment of Af-ghan hashish seized by undercover agents in 1987. At the same time the DEA arrested two men thought to be tied to a drug ring that smuggled hashish from Afghanistan and India into North America.

FIVE

Special Programs and Task Forces

The DEA uses a number of specially designed systems to gather, store, manage, and communicate information. All of these systems rely on sophisticated computer technology. Some are operated by the Office of Intelligence; others are operated by the Office of Science and Technology. The most important among them are the following:

- DEA Automated Teleprocessing System (DATS): An international communications system that, using telephone lines, gives agents in the United States and abroad instant access to many of the DEA's intelligence files, including such information as biographical and criminal records of suspects.

- DEA Communications: A nationwide radio and Teletype system that links the DEA with the Department of State and the Department of Defense.

- Narcotics and Dangerous Drugs Information System (NADDIS): A data base of more than 2 million records on people, businesses, ships, and airfields that are believed to be connected with criminal activities. The system is linked with the FBI's National Crime Information Center, Wanted Persons File, and Stolen Gun File.

- Pathfinder II: A centralized file of enforcement intelligence similar to NADDIS but smaller and available to non-DEA federal, state, or local drug enforcement authorities.

- System to Retrieve Information from Drug Evidence (STRIDE): A file of all information gathered by the DEA's forensic laboratories, useful for studying trends in drug abuse and trafficking and for estimating the availability and purity of street drugs.

- Precursor Chemical Information System (PCIS): Records of sales of precursors, as the raw materials used in the manufacture of some drugs are called. Precursor sales that are not accounted for by legitimately produced drugs may be a tip-off to the location of an underground lab.

- Controlled Substances Act System: A data base that contains all of the registrations required of legitimate drug producers and handlers under the Controlled Substances Act of 1970.

- Automated Reports and Consummated Orders System (ARCOS): A data base that contains reports from importers, manufacturers, distributors, and wholesalers who are authorized to handle controlled substances. This information is used to set quotas for the production of medical drugs and to alert investigators to possible illegal diversions.

- Drug Theft Reporting System (DTRS): Information about thefts or losses of controlled substances from registered handlers.

- Enforcement Management Information System (EMIS): A program that can evaluate individual investigations for current activity, status, use of agents, use of informants, and cost.

- Offender Based Transaction System (OBTS): A statistical system that uses information from the Bureau of Prisons to track the movements of drug violators through the justice system.

- DEA Accounting System (DEAAS II): An accounting program that keeps track of the DEA's funds and expenditures, produces financial reports, and is used to prepare budgets.

- Drug Abuse Warning Network (DAWN): A program shared by the DEA and the National Institute on Drug Abuse that uses reports from hospital emergency rooms, coroners, and crisis centers in selected cities to determine what drugs pose the greatest health hazards at a given time or place and to follow trends and changes in the pattern of drug abuse. One indicator of the crack crisis, for example, was the 86 percent increase in cocaine-related admissions to certain emergency rooms from 1986 to 1987.

The DEA uses a number of specially designed computer systems to gather, store, manage, and communicate information. Frequently it shares the information it compiles with other federal law enforcement agencies, state and local police forces, and drug enforcement officials in other countries.

The DEA also participates in a number of special interagency operations to meet particular drug enforcement needs. The most important of these are the marijuana suppression and eradication program, the financial investigations program, state and local task forces, administration initiatives, and the El Paso Intelligence Center.

Marijuana Suppression

Although DEA investigations are aimed at high-level narcotics dealers, the agency also contributes to the attack on marijuana cultivation within the United States. State and local drug enforcers, together with such federal agencies as

A field of marijuana bursts into flames, the result of a joint law enforcement effort to eliminate the trade in homegrown marijuana. As part of its marijuana-suppression program the DEA provides intelligence, training, aircraft, and occasional investigative help to such federal agencies as the Forest Service and the Bureau of Land Management and to state and local drug enforcement organizations.

the Forest Service, the Bureau of Alcohol, Tobacco and Firearms, and the Bureau of Land Management, are trying to wipe out the homegrown marijuana crop. The DEA provides these authorities with intelligence, training, aircraft and other equipment, and occasional investigative help. The program, which was initiated in 1981, destroyed more than 24 million marijuana plants by the beginning of 1988.

Financial Investigations

DEA employees who are trained in accounting and financial law work with members of the Internal Revenue Service, the U.S. Customs Service, and the FBI to trace international cash flows and to identify the assets of high-level drug dealers. This program has enabled enforcement officials to close in on traffickers who keep themselves isolated from actual contact with the drugs.

One extremely important aspect of the financial investigations program is called asset forfeiture. Under the Controlled Substances Act, the Racketeer Influenced and Corrupt Organizations (RICO) Act of 1961, and Public Law 98-473 of 1984, the profits of illicit trafficking by convicted drug dealers can be confiscated by U.S. law enforcement authorities. Such assets do not have to be in the form of cash; they can be boats, airplanes, buildings, stocks and bonds,

A luxury yacht is brought into the Miami Beach Coast Guard station after marijuana was discovered on board. Under U.S. law, federal law enforcement authorities can confiscate the property of drug dealers if they can show that the goods were purchased with the profits from illicit drug sales.

jewelry, and even entire businesses—as long as the investigators can show that they were purchased with the profits from illicit drug sales.

The possibility that drug bosses will have to forfeit their ill-gotten assets has hurt the drug trade in two ways. First, many dealers and smugglers are less willing to risk arrest and a prison term if there is a good chance that their riches will not be waiting for them when they get out. Second, asset forfeiture makes it harder for drug rings to keep operating if even a single high-level member is convicted and takes a big chunk of the ring's assets with him.

State and Local Task Forces

DEA special agents are sometimes assigned to task forces with state and local law enforcement officials. With DEA guidance, these task forces can strike fast and hard against mid-level drug violators, such as brokers (who act as middlemen between drug suppliers and retailers) and wholesalers (who buy drugs from brokers and sell them either to small-time retailers or directly to users). The task forces have a high arrest rate, and their rate of conviction in federal or state courts is more than 95 percent—in other words, they get results. By 1988, DEA agents were participating in state or local task forces in several dozen localities.

Administration Initiatives

Some of the DEA's special operations are the result of directions or proposals from the White House, the president's cabinet, or other high-ranking members of the administration.

For example, since the early 1980s the FBI and the DEA have worked together in a series of organized crime drug enforcement (OCDE) task forces created and headed by the attorney general. The purpose of these task forces is to bring down the top bosses of criminal organizations that deal in drugs, whether or not these individuals are directly involved in the drug traffic. Approximately 350 DEA employees—mostly special agents, although a few intelligence analysts and other specialists are also involved—are currently assigned to OCDE task forces.

Another administration initiative is the South Florida Task Force, which was founded by Vice-president George Bush in 1982. This task force unites representatives of the DEA, the U.S. Coast Guard, the U.S. Customs Service, the FBI, and other law enforcement groups. Its principal task is to curb the

Leon Kellner, the U.S. Attorney for the Southern District of Florida, announces the indictment on February 5, 1988, of Panamanian general Manuel Noriega on charges of assisting the Medellín cartel of Colombia in smuggling cocaine into the United States. The DEA has concentrated its antidrug efforts on arresting the key figures active in the drug trade, whether or not these individuals are directly involved in drug trafficking.

In November 1987, DEA and U.S. Customs agents in Miami, Florida, inter-cepted a 6,292-pound shipment of cocaine that was hidden inside the wooden slats of shipping crates. Florida's more than 1,000 miles of coastline and its proximity to South American drug sources make the state a major point of entry for illicit drugs.

New York City officials display $1.5 million in crack and about $500,000 in cocaine powder seized by drug agents during an October 1986 drug raid.

heavy flow of drugs, especially cocaine, into the Miami area. The task force concentrates on investigating air and sea smuggling, but it also conducts financial investigations into criminal organizations in the region.

The National Narcotics Border Interdiction System (NNBIS) is modeled on the South Florida Task Force. Its nationwide, multiagency effort is aimed at interdiction, which, in drug enforcement terms, means stopping illicit substances before they enter the country. The DEA contribution to the NNBIS consists of both intelligence and special agents on investigative assignments.

El Paso Intelligence Center

Founded in 1974 in El Paso, Texas, the El Paso Intelligence Center (EPIC) is a clearinghouse for drug information, especially up-to-the-minute information about drug movements that can be used to interdict smuggled narcotics. It is also used to track and interdict illegal aliens and smuggled weapons.

The El Paso Intelligence Center is a cooperative effort, with information provided by and shared among nine federal agencies: the DEA, the FBI, the

A worker at the El Paso Intelligence Center (EPIC) tracks the movement of illegal drugs on a map. Founded in 1974, EPIC is a clearinghouse for drug information and is staffed and run by the employees of nine federal agencies.

Internal Revenue Service, the U.S. Marshals Service, the Bureau of Alcohol, Tobacco and Firearms, the U.S. Coast Guard, the U.S. Customs Service, the Immigration and Naturalization Service, and the Federal Aviation Administration. The staff of EPIC is made up of representatives of all these agencies. In addition, EPIC has agreed to make its data bases available to the governments of all 50 states and of Puerto Rico and the Virgin Islands.

DEA Publications

Divisions and offices within the DEA produce or contribute to a variety of publications for drug enforcement use or for the general public. Many of these are technical manuals, articles, journals, or pamphlets that deal with forensic chemistry or intelligence reports.

But a number of DEA publications are written for nontechnical audiences. One such publication is the 16-page booklet "Drugs of Abuse," which identifies the drugs that are controlled by the DEA and describes the different forms of drug abuse. "Terms and Symptoms of Drug Abuse" is a poster that lists the effects of drug abuse on the body and mind. "A Community Program Guide: Drug Abuse Prevention" is aimed at community and social-service organizations and contains plans for an antidrug information program that such groups can put into action. The book *Drug Taking in Youth* is about the growth of drug abuse among American youngsters. It focuses on the psychological and social reasons for drug abuse and is aimed at parents, teachers, and social-service workers.

The DEA also produces a booklet of guidelines for the Explorers, part of the Boy Scouts of America, on preventing drug abuse, and a handbook called "School Drug Abuse Policy Guidelines" for educators and community leaders. It produces a manual for pharmacists on preventing drug thefts and one for physicians that explains the Controlled Substances Act. These publications are available in large public libraries, in government publications bookstores, or from the Office of Public Affairs, Drug Enforcement Administration, Department of Justice, 1405 I Street NW, Washington, DC, 20537 (202-633-1469). Finally, the DEA encourages children to be knowledgeable about drugs by contributing information and funds to antidrug programs such as the television cartoon show "Cops."

DEA agents seize a suspected drug dealer. Some experts contend that the war on drugs cannot be won through force but will only be won through widespread education about the dangers of drugs.

SIX

The DEA Today and Tomorrow

The drug problem is young. It has been less than a century since the United States began to regard narcotics as something dangerous, something from which people needed protection by law. The job of enforcing the drug laws that were passed fell to a number of federal organizations. Since 1973, when the government recognized that the drug problem had turned into a life-and-death issue, this job has belonged to the DEA—with help from an array of other federal, state, local, and foreign bodies.

The DEA has hurt the illicit drug trade in a number of ways. In 1988, it seized more than $655 million in drug traffickers' assets. Investigations by other agencies assisted by the DEA added another $198 million. This $853 million sum was a big loss to the drug trade and probably put some dealers out of business forever. It also made a healthy contribution to the U.S. Treasury, and the confiscated boats and airplanes can be used by drug agents to chase new smugglers.

Also in 1988, the DEA seized several billion dollars' worth of drugs before they reached the U.S. market: 55,897 kilograms of cocaine, 794 kilograms of heroin, 532,014 kilograms of cannabis products (hashish and marijuana), and

(continued on page 88)

Death of a DEA Agent

Late at night on February 28, 1989, a New York ex-convict named Constabile "Gus" Farace became the most-wanted man in the United States and the target of an intensive manhunt by 500 federal law enforcement agents. Farace was urgently sought for questioning as the number one suspect in the murder of DEA agent Everett Hatcher.

Hatcher, 46, married, and the father of two small children, was a special agent in the DEA's New York City division office on West 57th Street. At the time of his death he was working with other DEA and FBI agents on the investigation of a drug ring that was transporting cocaine from Florida to Staten Island, New York. Working undercover, Hatcher had already bought a small quantity of cocaine from Farace and now wanted to set up a one-kilogram buy. He arranged a meeting with Farace on a lonely dead-end Staten Island street, and he left for the meeting feeling confident. When a fellow agent offered to go with him, Hatcher said he could handle it alone. "No drugs, no money, just talk," he said. "It's a piece of cake."

But something went wrong—no one knows what. Five backup agents in three separate cars followed Hatcher, eavesdropping on his conversation with Farace and another hood by means of a concealed microphone that Hatcher wore taped under his shirt. Hatcher reported that he was following Farace to a nearby restaurant to talk business, but the backup team lost Farace's van and Hatcher's car at a red light. Then Hatcher's radio stopped transmitting. A frantic search of every restaurant parking lot along the road failed to turn up Hatcher's Buick. The agents' anxiety mounted, and finally one of them gave voice to what all must have been thinking: "Hatch is dead," he said. "We're going to find him dead." They did find him soon after, with his car's engine running, his foot on the brake, his machine gun locked in the trunk—and two bullet holes in his head. There was no sign of Farace.

Gus Farace's criminal career parallels that of the hundreds of violent young thugs and gunmen who have recently moved into the lower ranks of the old criminal organizations. In 1979, he and another minor criminal had attacked two men in a Staten Island park, beating one of them to death with a baseball bat. Farace was sentenced to prison for manslaughter and while in jail cultivated the friendship of a mobster named Gerard Chilli, who is believed to be an important figure in the Bonanno crime family. Farace served only seven years in prison, and authorities believe that he began dealing cocaine for Chilli in Staten Island immediately upon his release. Just eight months later, Hatcher's fatal meeting with Farace took place.

Slain DEA agent Everett Hatcher.

More than a month after the shooting, the 28-year-old Farace still had not been found.

Tragic in itself, Hatcher's death was also a disturbing reminder of the dangers faced by all drug agents. In the six months that preceded it, the New York office of the DEA alone had suffered grievous losses: Three agents had been shot, one agent had committed suicide, and the division head, Robert Stutman, was living under the threat of assassination because the cocaine cartel of Medellín, Colombia, had taken out a $1 million contract on his life after his agents confiscated a 7,500-pound cocaine shipment. Many agents be-gan to feel almost nostalgic for the mobsters of earlier decades, who were reluctant to incite federal law enforcement authorities by committing acts of violence against U.S. agents.

The Hatcher case made headlines around the nation and brought a flurry of attention and publicity to the DEA and its activities. It also brought newly inaugurated president George Bush to New York City to call on Hatcher's family and to visit Stutman's office. (Bush was the first president to visit a DEA field office.) Stutman hopes that the publicity that followed Hatcher's death will result in renewed public support for the DEA—and that that support might eventually take the form of increased federal funds for additional agents and antidrug programs. But although Stutman has been devoted to drug-law enforcement since 1965, he believes that targeting dealers is not enough to win the war on drugs. "No matter how good we get," he declares, "we will never be able to stop all the drugs. That's why law enforcement can't solve this problem—we need long-range prevention, and the best way to do that is through a mandatory K-through-12 drug education program in every school." For now, however, the undercover work of Everett Hatcher's fellow DEA agents continues to be the government's leading weapon against drugs.

(continued from page 85)
103,132,890 doses of illegal pills or other dangerous drugs. Except for minute amounts that will be used as legal evidence or for research purposes, these drugs are destroyed as quickly as possible. DEA agents also discovered and shut down 810 illegal drug labs in 1988.

During the same year, the DEA arrested 23,972 people on drug charges. Officials hope for a large number of convictions—at least 13,485, which is the number of convictions against DEA-arrested drug violators that were handed down by judges and juries in 1988. And the arrests made in 1988 included some very important dealers, such as the 200 Sicilian Connection defendants. The DEA also caught up with Dennis Howard Marks in 1988. An American living in Spain, Marks was believed to be the biggest smuggler of marijuana and hashish in the world, responsible for 15 percent of all cannabis products that entered the United States. He called himself "the Marco Polo of pot" and claimed he was too smart to be busted. But he was wrong. A DEA agent in Miami said, "I don't think he ever expected the long arm of the DEA overseas."

U.S. Customs agents, in conjunction with the South Florida Task Force, patrol the Florida seacoast in their $150,000 boat, Blue Thunder. *Funds to purchase the boat derived from the sale of the confiscated property of drug smugglers.*

Clifton StrengthsFinder THEMES

ACHIEVER® — People exceptionally talented in the Achiever theme work hard and possess a great deal of stamina. They take immense satisfaction in being busy and productive.

ACTIVATOR® — People exceptionally talented in the Activator theme can make things happen by turning thoughts into action. They are often impatient.

ADAPTABILITY® — People exceptionally talented in the Adaptability theme prefer to go with the flow. They tend to be "now" people who take things as they come and discover the future one day at a time.

ANALYTICAL® — People exceptionally talented in the Analytical theme search for reasons and causes. They have the ability to think about all the factors that might affect a situation.

ARRANGER® — People exceptionally talented in the Arranger theme can organize, but they also have a flexibility that complements this ability. They like to determine how all of the pieces and resources can be arranged for maximum productivity.

BELIEF® — People exceptionally talented in the Belief theme have certain core values that are unchanging. Out of these values emerges a defined purpose for their lives.

COMMAND® — People exceptionally talented in the Command theme have presence. They can take control of a situation and make decisions.

COMMUNICATION® — People exceptionally talented in the Communication theme generally find it easy to put their thoughts into words. They are good conversationalists and presenters.

COMPETITION® — People exceptionally talented in the Competition theme measure their progress against the performance of others. They strive to win first place and revel in contests.

CONNECTEDNESS® — People exceptionally talented in the Connectedness theme have faith in the links among all things. They believe there are few coincidences and that almost every event has meaning.

CONSISTENCY™ — People exceptionally talented in the Consistency theme are keenly aware of the need to treat people the same. They try to treat everyone with equality by setting up clear rules and adhering to them.

CONTEXT® — People exceptionally talented in the Context theme enjoy thinking about the past. They understand the present by researching its history.

DELIBERATIVE™ — People exceptionally talented in the Deliberative theme are best described by the serious care they take in making decisions or choices. They anticipate obstacles.

DEVELOPER® — People exceptionally talented in the Developer theme recognize and cultivate the potential in others. They spot the signs of each small improvement and derive satisfaction from evidence of progress.

DISCIPLINE™ — People exceptionally talented in the Discipline theme enjoy routine and structure. Their world is best described by the order they create.

EMPATHY™ — People exceptionally talented in the Empathy theme can sense other people's feelings by imagining themselves in others' lives or situations.

FOCUS™ — People exceptionally talented in the Focus theme can take a direction, follow through, and make the corrections necessary to stay on track. They prioritize, then act.

FUTURISTIC® — People exceptionally talented in the Futuristic theme are inspired by the future and what could be. They energize others with their visions of the future.

HARMONY® — People exceptionally talented in the Harmony theme look for consensus. They don't enjoy conflict; rather, they seek areas of agreement.

IDEATION® — People exceptionally talented in the Ideation theme are fascinated by ideas. They are able to find connections between seemingly disparate phenomena.

INCLUDER® — People exceptionally talented in the Includer theme accept others. They show awareness of those who feel left out and make an effort to include them.

INDIVIDUALIZATION® — People exceptionally talented in the Individualization theme are intrigued with the unique qualities of each person. They have a gift for figuring out how different people can work together productively.

INPUT® — People exceptionally talented in the Input theme have a craving to know more. Often they like to collect and archive all kinds of information.

INTELLECTION® — People exceptionally talented in the Intellection theme are characterized by their intellectual activity. They are introspective and appreciate intellectual discussions.

LEARNER® — People exceptionally talented in the Learner theme have a great desire to learn and want to continuously improve. The process of learning, rather than the outcome, excites them.

MAXIMIZER® — People exceptionally talented in the Maximizer theme focus on strengths as a way to stimulate personal and group excellence. They seek to transform something strong into something superb.

POSITIVITY® — People exceptionally talented in the Positivity theme have contagious enthusiasm. They are upbeat and can get others excited about what they are going to do.

RELATOR® — People exceptionally talented in the Relator theme enjoy close relationships with others. They find deep satisfaction in working hard with friends to achieve a goal.

RESPONSIBILITY® — People exceptionally talented in the Responsibility theme take psychological ownership of what they say they will do. They are committed to stable values such as honesty and loyalty.

RESTORATIVE™ — People exceptionally talented in the Restorative theme are adept at dealing with problems. They are good at figuring out what is wrong and resolving it.

SELF-ASSURANCE® — People exceptionally talented in the Self-Assurance theme feel confident in their ability to manage their own lives. They possess an inner compass that gives them confidence that their decisions are right.

SIGNIFICANCE™ — People exceptionally talented in the Significance theme want to be very important in others' eyes. They are independent and want to be recognized.

STRATEGIC™ — People exceptionally talented in the Strategic theme create alternative ways to proceed. Faced with any given scenario, they can quickly spot the relevant patterns and issues.

WOO™ — People exceptionally talented in the Woo theme love the challenge of meeting new people and winning them over. They derive satisfaction from breaking the ice and making a connection with someone.

Problems and Challenges

In spite of these achievements and victories, the DEA is fighting an uphill battle in the war on drugs. There are so many users and so many people desperate to make a living scratching opium or coca out of the ground—and so many others eager to risk death or imprisonment to make a huge fortune in the trade—that no victory is complete.

The arrest of Dennis Howard Marks and 21 of his accomplices, for example, will probably destroy only half of Marks's smuggling empire, according to the DEA. And when the DEA sends agents and helicopters to Peru's Huallaga Valley to help destroy the coca crop, the peasant farmers move their fields higher up the mountainsides to altitudes where helicopters cannot function but coca thrives. The extradition in 1987 of drug smuggler Carlos Lehder Rivas from Colombia and his conviction on drug charges were triumphs for the DEA, but Pablo Escobar Gaviria and dozens of other cocaine kingpins remain untouched in Colombia. Furthermore, the Colombian courts recently overturned their country's extradition treaty with the United States. For every step forward, there is at least one step back.

The South Florida Task Force has concentrated on insulating Florida from the small aircraft that were the smugglers' vehicles of choice in the early 1980s. To a large extent it has succeeded, using a mix of radar balloons and air sweeps by the navy and the air force. But the drug runners have money and technology on their side. They have begun to cut through coastal waters in $100,000 fiberglass boats called "go-fasts." These boats, which cannot be detected by radar, are equipped with night-vision telescopes and top-quality radios and are capable of speeds of 80 miles per hour. Federal funds simply do not stretch far enough to equip drug officials with go-fasters. In 1988, smuggling was up in the Miami area.

In late 1988, DEA officials estimated that to make their strategy of targeting the world's top drug traffickers truly effective, they would need at least 2,500 more agents. The cost of such an increase in staff and operations would be about $1 billion over a 5-year period. But hundreds of other agencies and programs are jostling for funds. The DEA's budget will probably increase over the next five years—but not by a billion dollars.

Shortly before his inauguration in January 1989, President George Bush created a new advisory position in the executive branch of government—national drug control policy director. Bush appointed William J. Bennett, formerly the secretary of education under President Ronald Reagan, as the first drug chief. Bennett's task will be to form a unified policy that all federal drug enforcement agencies will help carry out. This task will not be an easy one. Some experts say that the best strategy in the war on drugs would be to concentrate on prevention—to educate people about the dangers of drugs and to spend more money on treatment for addicts and users. Others claim that the best approach would be to scare the public out of the drug habit by arresting and jailing every single user and small-time dealer, but the nation's court and prison systems could not begin to meet such a demand. Still others, the DEA and the FBI among them, maintain that the top priority must be breaking up the drug traffic at its highest levels. Unless and until a different policy is agreed on, that is what the DEA will continue to do.

Some of the challenges that the DEA faces in the immediate future are easy to see. Cocaine, and its derivative crack, will continue to be public enemy number one. Efforts will continue to extradite the leaders of the Colombian cartels—but the enforcement experts are not optimistic. DEA activity in Mexico has increased enormously since a DEA agent and his pilot were tortured to death there in 1985. And Mexico will certainly be high on the DEA's priority list in the 1990s, as current investigations suggest that there may be a massive network of drug-related corruption in the Mexican government.

National drug control policy director William J. Bennett (left) meets with President George Bush in February 1989. One of Bennett's first initiatives was to announce a multi-million-dollar federal plan to combat the drug menace in Washington, D.C.

The body of DEA agent Enrique Camarena, who was tortured to death in Mexico in 1985, arrives at the North Island Naval Air Station in San Diego, California. For every step forward in the war on drugs often there is one step backward.

During one drug bust in April 1988, approximately 80 Mexican police officers were taken into custody on charges of assisting Miguel Angel Félix Gallardo, the country's foremost trafficker of cocaine. Félix Gallardo, who is believed to be the leader of an international drug ring responsible for shipping up to two tons of cocaine to the United States every month, was also arrested. Although the DEA welcomed the news of Félix Gallardo's capture and believed it would have a significant effect on the drug trade in that region of Mexico, the drug trafficker's arrest is just a small victory in a very large war.

No doubt new and unforeseen challenges will arise: Perhaps new strains of coca plants that can be grown in a wider geographical range will be developed. Or perhaps new smuggling routes will emerge that will require agents to be shifted around the country—or around the world. DEA agents know that the war on drugs will not be won easily or soon. They simply work to win as many of the battles as they can.

Drug Enforcement Administration

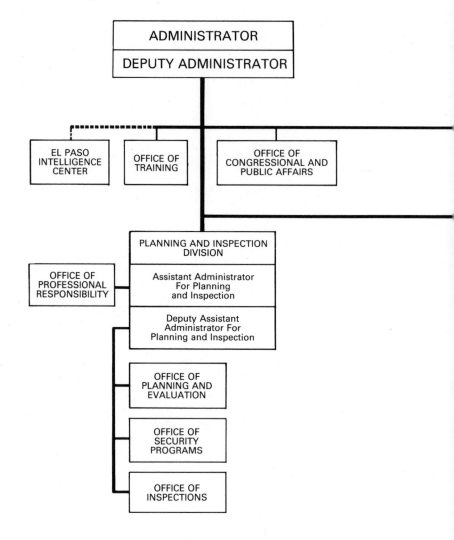

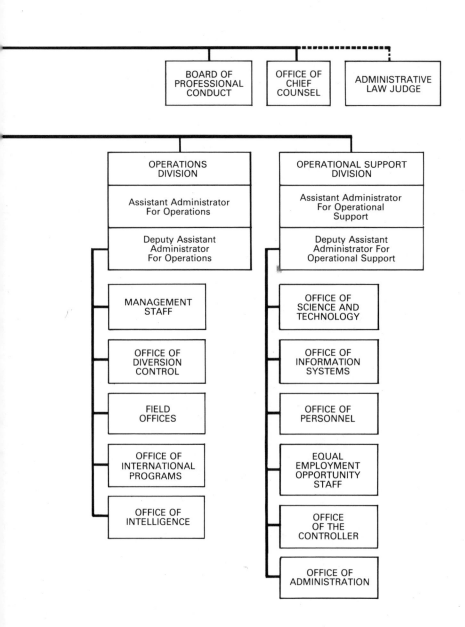

BOARD OF PROFESSIONAL CONDUCT

OFFICE OF CHIEF COUNSEL

ADMINISTRATIVE LAW JUDGE

OPERATIONS DIVISION

Assistant Administrator For Operations

Deputy Assistant Administrator For Operations

MANAGEMENT STAFF

OFFICE OF DIVERSION CONTROL

FIELD OFFICES

OFFICE OF INTERNATIONAL PROGRAMS

OFFICE OF INTELLIGENCE

OPERATIONAL SUPPORT DIVISION

Assistant Administrator For Operational Support

Deputy Assistant Administrator For Operational Support

OFFICE OF SCIENCE AND TECHNOLOGY

OFFICE OF INFORMATION SYSTEMS

OFFICE OF PERSONNEL

EQUAL EMPLOYMENT OPPORTUNITY STAFF

OFFICE OF THE CONTROLLER

OFFICE OF ADMINISTRATION

Appendix:
DEA Division Offices

Atlanta Office
75 Spring Street SW
Atlanta, GA   30303

Boston Office
John F. Kennedy Office Building
Boston, MA   02203

Chicago Office
219 S. Dearborn Street
Chicago, IL   60604

Dallas Office
1880 Regal Row
Dallas, TX   75235

Denver Office
316 U.S. Customs House
Denver, CO   80201

Detroit Office
231 W. Lafayette
Detroit, MI   48226

Houston Office
333 W. Loop Street
Houston, TX   77024

Los Angeles Office
350 S. Figueroa Street
Los Angeles, CA   90071

Miami Office
8400 NW 53rd Street
Miami, FL   33166

Newark Office
970 Broad Street
Newark, NJ   07102

New Orleans Office
1661 Canal Street
New Orleans, LA   70112

New York Office
555 W. 57th Street
New York, NY   10019

Philadelphia Office
600 Arch Street
Philadelphia, PA   19106

Phoenix Office
1 N. First
Phoenix, AZ   85004

San Diego Office
402 W. 35th Street
San Diego, CA   92050

San Francisco Office
450 Golden Gate Avenue
San Francisco, CA   94102

Seattle Office
220 W. Mercer
Seattle, WA   98119

St. Louis Office
7911 Forsyth Boulevard
St. Louis, MO   63105

Washington Office
400 6th Street SW
Washington, DC   20024

GLOSSARY

Addiction   Physical dependence on a drug, in which the individual cannot function normally without repeated dosages of the drug and suffers severe physical and mental disturbances if the drug is withdrawn.

Amphetamines   Drugs that act as stimulants on the central nervous system.

Asset forfeiture   The confiscation (permitted by federal law) of the property of drug dealers, amassed through illicit drug trafficking, by U.S. law-enforcement authorities. These assets often include cash, boats, airplanes, stocks and bonds, and entire businesses.

Bagman   An individual working for a drug cartel who collects profits from wholesale dealers.

Barbiturates   Any of the various derivatives of barbituric acid used especially as sedatives, hypnotics, and antispasmodics.

Bootlegger   Someone who illegally manufactures, sells, or transports a product, such as alcohol.

Broker   An individual, almost always operating within a criminal organization, who serves as a middleman between drug suppliers and retailers and who arranges for the sale and distribution of drugs to wholesale dealers throughout the country.

Cannabis sativa   A member of the hemp family of flowering plants. Its leaves and stems are consumed as marijuana, and its resins are consumed as hashish. Both of these drugs are habit-forming intoxicants, with hashish being the more concentrated and stronger.

Coca   A plant native to western South America from whose leaves the drug cocaine is produced. Inhabitants of the region chew coca leaves for their stimulating and painkilling properties.

Cocaine   *See* Coca.

Codeine   *See* Opium.

Courier   An individual who transports or delivers drugs, often across national borders, from suppliers to retailers.

Crop eradication   The destruction of coca, opium, and marijuana plants by chemical spraying or fire. Often the DEA teams up with authorities at the local, state, federal, and international levels in its activities in this area.

Crop substitution   Programs that encourage or pay farmers to grow legal, rather than drug-producing, crops.

Customs agent   A government official, working at an international airport or border station, whose responsibilities include inspecting people and packages entering or exiting a country in order to prevent the flow of drugs across national borders.

Crack   A form of cocaine that can be smoked.

Drug   A substance whose chemical nature alters the structure or function of a living organism. In terms of law enforcement, a chemical that affects human mood, perception, or consciousness and can be injurious to the individual and to society.

Drug ballistics   A highly specialized form of drug analysis that uses microscopically precise measurements and chemical analyses to identify the original source of a powder or pill.

Drug cartel   A drug organization that has its own network of chemists, accountants, gunmen, and other personnel.

Geographic Drug Enforcement Program (G-DEP)   A DEA investigation system used to classify drug violators according to the type and amount of drugs involved, the area affected by criminal operation, and the violator's position in the criminal organization.

Habituation   An addiction formed after frequent repetition or prolonged use of something, such as drugs.

Hallucinogen   A drug, either synthetic or naturally occurring, that causes hallucinations, or illusions of seeing something that does not exist. Lysergic acid diethylamide (LSD), mescaline, peyote, psilocybin, and phencyclidine (PCP) are the most common hallucinogens.

Hashish   See *Cannabis sativa.*

Hemp   A fibrous plant from which the psychoactive drugs marijuana and hashish are derived.

Heroin   *See* Opium.

International Criminal Police Organization (Interpol)   A multi-national group that coordinates the exchange of information between criminal investigation departments of its member nations.

Intelligence   Secret information, especially about an enemy or opponent, that is an important component of both espionage and law-enforcement operations; also the process of gathering this information.

Morphine   *See* Opium.

Narcotic   A habit-forming drug that produces unconsciousness or sleep or reduces pain. In law enforcement the term is generally used to refer to opium-based or coca-based drugs, although coca drugs are more often stimulating than relaxing in their effect.

Opium   The concentrated sap of the flower of the opium poppy. In its raw form, opium is a powerful narcotic that can be eaten, smoked, or consumed in a liquid; in small doses, it has some medicinal uses. It can be chemically processed into the narcotics morphine, a powerful sleeping drug and painkiller; codeine, also a painkiller; and heroin, which has no known medical properties.

Soma   An opium-based beverage, sometimes containing alcohol, used in many early Asian cultures.

Wholesaler   An individual who buys drugs from brokers and sells them either to small-time retailers or directly to users.

World Health Organization   A group that advises and trains people in health administration, coordinates projects to combat widespread disease, and studies drug use throughout the world.

SELECTED REFERENCES

Allen, William A., Nicholas L. Piccone, and Christopher D'Amada. *How Drugs Can Affect Your Life.* Springfield, IL: Thomas, 1983.

Bakalar, James B., and Lester Grinspoon. *Drug Control in a Free Society.* Cambridge: Cambridge University Press, 1984.

Dunn, Lynne. *The Department of Justice.* New York: Chelsea House, 1989.

Ferguson, Robert W. *Drug Abuse Control.* Boston: Holbrook Press, 1975.

Goddard, Donald. *Undercover: The Lives of a Federal Agent.* New York: Times Books, 1988.

Gugliotta, Guy, and Jeff Leen. *Kings of Cocaine: Inside the Medellín Cartel—An Astonishing True Story of Murder, Money, and International Corruption.* New York: Simon & Schuster, 1989.

Inglis, Brian. *The Forbidden Game: A Social History of Drugs.* New York: Scribners, 1975.

Kiev, Ari. *The Drug Epidemic.* New York: Free Press, 1975.

Musto, David F. *The American Disease: Origins of Narcotic Control.* New York: Oxford University Press, 1988.

Pooley, Eric. "A Federal Case," *New York,* March 27, 1989, 46–58.

INDEX

Drug Enforcement Administration (*cont.*)
  founding of, 27, 49
  international offices of, 60
  mission of, 57
  organizational change in, 50, 54
  publications of, 83
  special agents of, 66, 69, 71
  staff of, 57–58
  task forces of, 78, 81, 89
Drug Investigations Unit, 49
Drug Theft Reporting System (DTRS), 74

El Paso Intelligence Center (EPIC), 81, 83
Enforcement Management Information System (EMIS), 74
Erythroxylon coca. See Coca, Cocaine, Crack
Europe, 19, 31, 32, 33

Farace, Constabile "Gus," 86, 87
Federal Bureau of Investigation (FBI), 15, 16, 19, 25, 49, 50, 54, 60, 63, 65, 68, 69, 77, 78, 81, 90
Federal Law Enforcement Training Center (FLETC), 65
Food and Drug Administration (FDA), 27, 39, 46, 63
Forest Service, 76
Freud, Sigmund, 33

Gallardo, Miguel Angel Félix, 91
Gaviria, Pablo Escobar, 53, 89
Geographic Drug Enforcement Program (G-DEP), 54, 55, 64
Goddard, Donald, 66
Great Britain, 32

Habituation, 43
Hague Opium Convention, 35

Hallucinogens, 22, 31, 39
Harrison Narcotics Act of 1914, 35, 36
Hashish, 22, 31, 39, 85, 88
Hatcher, Everett, 86, 87
Heroin, 15, 17, 18, 19, 21, 22, 23, 33, 38, 39, 44, 60, 85
Holmes, Sherlock, 33, 34
Huallaga Valley, 52, 89

Ibuprofen, 46
Iliad (Homer), 29
Indians, 31
Indonesia, 35
Interdiction, 81
Internal Revenue Service (IRS), 36, 39, 77, 83
International Criminal Police Organization (Interpol), 27, 57
Italy, 15, 16, 18, 19

Justice, Department of, 23, 41, 49, 54

Latin America, 21
Laudanum, 32
Levine, Michael, 66–67
LSD, 39, 44, 46

Marijuana, 21, 22, 31, 39, 44, 55, 63, 75, 76, 85, 88
Marijuana Tax Act of 1937, 39
Marks, Dennis Howard, 88, 89
Medellín, Colombia, 53, 87
Mescaline, 39, 44
Mesopotamia, 29
Methadone, 46
Methamphetamine, 46
Methaqualone, 44
Mexico, 35, 60, 90, 91
Miami, Florida, 59, 60, 81, 89
Morphine, 32, 33, 34, 38, 39, 46

Narcotic Control Act of 1956, 39

Rebecca Stefoff is a Philadelphia-based writer and editor. She holds a Ph.D. in English from the University of Philadelphia, where she taught for three years. Ms. Stefoff is the author of more than 30 books of biography and nonfiction for young adults, including *The U.S. Coast Guard* in Chelsea House's KNOW YOUR GOVERNMENT series. Currently she is the editorial director of the Chelsea House series PLACES AND PEOPLES OF THE WORLD.

Arthur M. Schlesinger, jr., served in the White House as special assistant to Presidents Kennedy and Johnson. He is the author of numerous acclaimed works in American history and has twice been awarded the Pulitzer Prize. He taught history at Harvard College for many years and is currently Albert Schweitzer Professor of the Humanities at the City College of New York.

PICTURE CREDITS